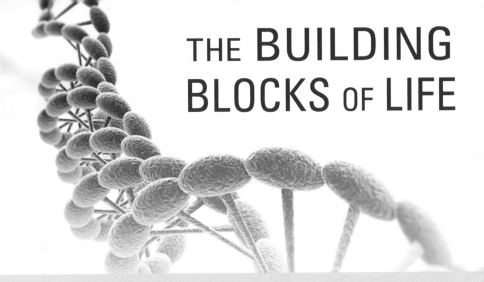

THE BUILDING BLOCKS OF LIFE

EXAMINING VIRUSES AND BACTERIA

Edited by **Louise Eaton** and **Kara Rogers**

Britannica
Educational Publishing

IN ASSOCIATION WITH

ROSEN
EDUCATIONAL SERVICES

Published in 2018 by Britannica Educational Publishing (a trademark of Encyclopædia Britannica, Inc.) in association with The Rosen Publishing Group, Inc.
29 East 21st Street, New York, NY 10010

Distributed exclusively by Rosen Publishing.
To see additional Britannica Educational Publishing titles, go to rosenpublishing.com.

Britannica Educational Publishing
J. E. Luebering: Executive Director, Core Editorial
Andrea R. Field: Managing Editor, Compton's by Britannica

Rosen Publishing
Meredith Day: Editor
Nelson Sá: Art Director
Brian Garvey: Series Designer
Ellina Litmanovich: Book Layout
Cindy Reiman: Photography Manager
Nicole DiMella: Photo Researcher

Library of Congress Cataloging-in-Publication Data

Names: Eaton, Louise, editor. | Rogers, Kara, editor.
Title: Examining viruses and bacteria / edited by Louise Eaton and Kara Rogers.
Description: New York : Britannica Educational Publishing, in Association with Rosen Educational Services, 2018. | Series: The building blocks of life | Audience: Grades 9–12. | Includes bibliographical references and index.
Identifiers: LCCN 2017011860 | ISBN 9781538300091 (library bound : alk. paper)
Subjects: LCSH: Viruses—Juvenile literature. | Bacteria—Juvenile literature.
Classification: LCC QR365 .E93 2018 | DDC 579.3/165—dc23
LC record available at https://lccn.loc.gov/2017011860

Manufactured in Malaysia

CONTENTS

CHAPTER 3

INTRODUCTION

I n the hidden world of microscopic things, bacteria and viruses are among the most amazing and the most mysterious. Knowledge of the existence of life invisible to the naked eye first emerged in the 17th century, with the invention of the microscope by Dutch microscopist Antonie van Leeuwenhoek. Among the various types of "animalcules," or little animals, that Leeuwenhoek discovered with the aid of his microscope were the single-celled organisms now known as bacteria.

In Leeuwenhoek's time, these microscopic forms were the subjects of intense scientific debate. Prior to bacteria, scientists had hypothesized that living organisms developed from nonliving matter in a process called spontaneous generation. In the 19th century, however, spontaneous generation was overturned by French chemist and microbiologist Louis Pasteur, whose research on bacteria published in 1861 helped to establish the principle of biogenesis—that organisms arise only through the reproduction of other organisms. Biogenesis also

supported germ theory, the idea that disease can arise as a result of invasion of the body by microorganisms. Biogenesis and germ theory represented the very early stages of scientists' understanding of bacteria, and in subsequent decades far more became known about these amazing microbes, particularly concerning their roles in Earth's various ecosystems, such as contributing to the breakdown of organic matter in soils and sharing in symbiotic relationships with other organisms.

Bacteria are microscopic single-celled organisms that live in enormous numbers in almost every environment on the surface of Earth, from deep-sea vents to the digestive tracts of humans. They are characterized morphologically by the absence of a membrane-bound nucleus and other internal structures and are therefore ranked among the unicellular life-forms called prokaryotes. Prokaryotes are the dominant living creatures on Earth, having been present for perhaps three-quarters of Earth's history and having adapted to almost all available ecological habitats.

As a group, the bacteria display exceedingly diverse metabolic capabilities and can use almost any organic compound, and some inorganic compounds, as a food source. Some bacteria can cause diseases in humans, animals, or plants. Pathogenic bacteria may enter the body in many ways, such as through the mouth or through cuts in the skin. If they multiply sufficiently they can cause an infection. The infection may be caused by the microbes themselves, or by poisons called toxins that they produce. Some toxins, such as those produced by *Staphylococcus aureus*, are more dangerous than the bacteria. Plants, too, are vulnerable to bacterial infections, though they are plagued by different species than are animals.

However, most bacteria are harmless and are beneficial ecological agents whose metabolic activities sustain higher life-forms. Other bacteria are symbionts of plants and invertebrates, where they carry out important functions for the host, such as nitrogen fixation and cellulose degradation. Without prokaryotes, soil would not be fertile, and dead organic material would decay much more slowly. Some bacteria are widely used in the preparation of foods, chemicals, and antibiotics. Studies of the relationships between different groups of bacteria continue to yield new insights into the origin of life on Earth and the mechanisms of evolution.

As some bacteria and other microbes "digest" nutrients, they produce certain chemical products through a process called fermentation. Dairy products are fermented in many ways to produce products such as sour cream, buttermilk, cheese, and yogurt. Cheeses owe their various flavors almost entirely to different kinds of combinations of bacteria and mold. On the other hand, the bacteria that bring about decay are the chief cause of food spoilage.

Viruses are infectious agents of small size and simple composition that can multiply only in living cells of animals, plants, or bacteria. Their name is from a Latin word meaning "slimy liquid" or "poison." Researchers have long debated whether or not viruses are living or nonliving entities, since outside of a living cell a virus is an inactive particle, but within an appropriate host cell it becomes active, capable of taking over the cell's metabolic machinery for the production of new virus particles (virions). Most viruses inflict harm on host organisms, and there are a number of widespread pathogenic (disease-causing) viruses known to humans. Among these pathogens is human immunodeficiency virus (HIV), which causes acquired immune deficiency syndrome (AIDS), a disease in which the immune system is gradually destroyed, over the course of years, as a result of viral infection. The widespread transmission of HIV is of global concern, and despite tremendous efforts in drug discovery and medicine, a cure for infection is yet to be found.

The earliest indications of the biological nature

of viruses came from studies in 1892 by the Russian scientist Dmitry I. Ivanovsky and in 1898 by the Dutch scientist Martinus W. Beijerinck. Beijerinck first surmised that the virus under study was a new kind of infectious agent, which he designated *contagium vivum fluidum*, meaning that it was a live, reproducing organism that differed from other organisms. Both of these investigators found that a disease of tobacco plants could be transmitted by an agent, later called tobacco mosaic virus, passing through a minute filter that would not allow the passage of bacteria. This virus and those subsequently isolated would not grow on an artificial medium and were not visible under the light microscope. In independent studies in 1915 by the British investigator Frederick W. Twort and in 1917 by the French Canadian scientist Félix d'Hérelle, lesions in cultures of bacteria were discovered and attributed to an agent called bacteriophage ("eater of bacteria"), now known to be viruses that specifically infect bacteria.

The unique nature of these organisms meant that new methods and alternative models had to be developed to study and classify them. The study of viruses confined exclusively or largely to humans, however, posed the formidable problem of finding a susceptible animal host. In 1933 the British investigators Wilson Smith, Christopher H. Andrewes, and Patrick P. Laidlaw were able to transmit influenza to ferrets, and the influenza virus was subsequently adapted to mice. In 1941 the American scientist George K. Hirst found that influenza virus grown in tissues of the chicken embryo could be detected by its capacity to agglutinate (draw together) red blood cells.

A significant advance was made by the American scientists John Enders, Thomas Weller, and Frederick Robbins, who in 1949 developed the technique of culturing cells on glass surfaces; cells could then be infected with the viruses that cause polio (poliovirus) and other diseases. (Until this time, the poliovirus could be grown only in the brains of chimpanzees or the spinal cords of monkeys.) Culturing cells on glass surfaces opened the way for diseases caused by viruses to be identified by their effects on cells (cytopathogenic effect) and by the presence of antibodies to them in the blood. Cell culture then led to the development and production of vaccines (preparations used to elicit immunity against a disease) such as the poliovirus vaccine.

Scientists were soon able to detect the number of bacterial viruses in a culture vessel by measuring their ability to break apart (lyse) adjoining bacteria in an area of bacteria (lawn) overlaid with an inert gelatinous substance called agar—viral action that resulted in a clearing, or "plaque." The American scientist Renato Dulbecco in 1952 applied this technique to measuring the number of animal viruses that could produce plaques in layers of adjoining animal cells overlaid with agar. In the 1940s the development

John Enders, Thomas Weller, and Frederick Robbins won the Nobel Prize for Medicine or Physiology in 1954 for the successful cultivation of poliomyelitis virus in tissue cultures. Weller (*left*) and Enders are shown here at the Children's Medical Center in Boston in 1954.

of the electron microscope permitted individual virus particles to be seen for the first time, leading to the classification of viruses and giving insight into their structure.

Advancements that were made in chemistry, physics, and molecular biology since the 1960s have revolutionized the study of viruses. For example, electrophoresis on gel substrates gave a deeper understanding of the protein and nucleic acid composition of viruses. More sophisticated immunologic procedures, including the use of monoclonal antibodies directed to specific antigenic sites on proteins, gave a better insight into the structure and function of viral proteins. The progress made in the physics of crystals that could be studied by X-ray diffraction provided the high resolution required to discover the basic structure of minute viruses. Applications of new knowledge about cell biology and biochemistry helped to determine how viruses use their host cells for synthesizing viral nucleic acids and proteins.

The revolution that took place in the field of molecular biology allowed the genetic information encoded in nucleic acids of viruses—which enables viruses to reproduce, synthesize unique proteins, and alter cellular functions—to be studied. In fact, the chemical and physical simplicity of viruses has made them an incisive experimental tool for probing the molecular events involved in certain life processes.

Because the role of bacteria and viruses in human disease is so significant, microbiology—an area of study concerned with the structure, function, classification, and manipulation of microscopic entities—is at the forefront of modern science. Ongoing research efforts are focused largely on obtaining a better understanding of the distribution in nature of bacteria and viruses and their role in disease and on learning more about their evolution and natural histories. Indeed, the primitive ancestors of bacteria, known as the archaea, are believed to be representatives of some of Earth's earliest life-forms; studies have indicated that the first archaea appeared on Earth about 3.5 billion years ago, followed by the first bacteria, the cyanobacteria (blue-green algae), some 3 billion years ago. Although the evolution of viruses is much less clear, they are believed to have emerged about 200 million years ago. Thus, bacteria and viruses are significant not only for their role in disease but also for their role in the evolution of life on early Earth.

CHAPTER

1

FEATURES AND REPRODUCTION OF BACTERIA

All living organisms on Earth are made up of one of two basic types of cells: eukaryotic cells, in which the genetic material is enclosed within a nuclear membrane, or prokaryotic cells, in which the genetic material is not separated from the rest of the cell. Traditionally, all prokaryotic cells were called bacteria and were classified in the prokaryotic kingdom Monera. However, their classification as Monera, equivalent in taxonomy to the other kingdoms—Plantae, Animalia, Fungi, and Protista—understated the remarkable genetic and metabolic diversity exhibited by prokaryotic cells relative to eukaryotic cells. In the late 1970s American microbiologist Carl Woese pioneered a major change in classification by placing all organisms into three domains—Eukarya, Bacteria (originally

17

called Eubacteria), and Archaea (originally called Archaebacteria)—to reflect the three ancient lines of evolution. The prokaryotic organisms that were formerly known as bacteria were then divided into two of these domains, Bacteria and Archaea. Bacteria and Archaea are superficially similar; for example, they do not have intracellular organelles, and they have circular DNA. However, they are fundamentally distinct, and their separation is based on the genetic evidence for their ancient and separate evolutionary lineages, as well as fundamental differences in their chemistry and physiology. Members of these two prokaryotic domains are as different from one another as they are from eukaryotic cells.

Prokaryotic cells (i.e., Bacteria and Archaea) are fundamentally different from the eukaryotic cells that constitute other forms of life. Prokaryotic cells are defined by a much simpler design than is found in eukaryotic cells. The most apparent simplification is the lack of intracellular organelles, which are features characteristic of eukaryotic cells. Organelles are discrete membrane-enclosed structures that are contained in the cytoplasm and include the nucleus, where genetic information is retained, copied, and expressed; the mitochondria and chloroplasts, where chemical or light energy is converted into metabolic energy; the lysosome, where ingested proteins are digested and other nutrients are made available; and the endoplasmic reticulum and the

Golgi apparatus, where the proteins that are synthesized by and released from the cell are assembled, modified, and exported. All of the activities performed by organelles also take place in bacteria, but they are not carried out by specialized structures. In addition, prokaryotic cells are usually much smaller than eukaryotic cells. The small size, simple design, and broad metabolic capabilities of bacteria allow them to grow and divide very rapidly and to inhabit and flourish in almost any environment.

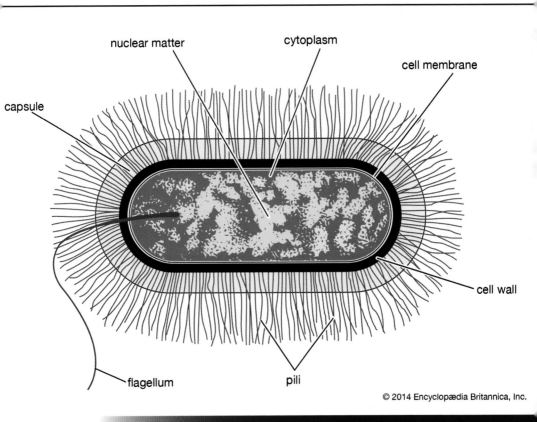

© 2014 Encyclopædia Britannica, Inc.

Schematic drawing of the structure of a typical bacterial cell of the *bacillus* (rodlike) type.

Prokaryotic and eukaryotic cells differ in many other ways, including lipid composition, structure of key metabolic enzymes, responses to antibiotics and toxins, and the mechanism of expression of genetic information. Eukaryotic organisms contain multiple linear chromosomes with genes that are much larger than they need to be to encode the synthesis of proteins. Substantial portions of the ribonucleic acid (RNA) copy of the genetic information (deoxyribonucleic acid, or DNA) are discarded, and the remaining messenger RNA (mRNA) is substantially modified before it is translated into protein. In contrast, bacteria have one circular chromosome that contains all of their genetic information, and their mRNAs are exact copies of their gene and are not modified.

SHAPE AND STRUCTURE

Although bacterial cells are much smaller and simpler in structure than eukaryotic cells, the bacteria are an exceedingly diverse group of organisms that differ in size, shape, habitat, and metabolism. Much of the knowledge about bacteria has come from studies of disease-causing bacteria, which are more readily isolated in pure culture and more easily investigated than are many of the free-living species of bacteria. It must be noted that many free-living bacteria are quite different from the bacteria that are adapted to live as animal parasites. Thus, there are no absolute

DISCOVERING ARCHAEA

American microbiologist Carl Woese (1928–2012) discovered the group of single-cell prokaryotic organisms known as archaea, which constitute a third domain of life.

Prior to 1977 and Woese's seminal paper in *Proceedings of the National Academy of Sciences*, many biologists believed that all life on Earth belonged to one of two primary lineages—the eukaryotes, which included animals, plants, fungi, and some single-cell organisms, and the prokaryotes, which included bacteria and all remaining microscopic organisms. Woese, working with American microbiologist Ralph S. Wolfe, determined that prokaryotes actually comprise two distinctly different groups of organisms and should be divided into two categories: true bacteria (eubacteria) and the newly recognized archaebacteria, later renamed archaea. Archaea are aquatic or terrestrial microorganisms that differ both biochemically and genetically from true bacteria. Many of these organisms thrive in extreme environments, including those that are very hot or that have a high degree of salinity. Some of these organisms live in the absence of oxygen and thus are described as being anaerobic. Because such conditions resemble Earth's early environment, archaea were thought to hold important information about the evolution of cells.

In 1996 Woese and colleagues from the University of Illinois and the Institute for Genomic Research in

(Continued on the next page)

(Continued from the previous page)

Rockville, Md., published the first complete genome, or full genetic blueprint, of an organism in the archaea domain and concluded that archaea are more closely related to eukaryotes than to bacteria. The publication of the genome helped to quell ongoing resistance to the idea of a third domain of life in the scientific community. In two papers that were published in 1998 and 2000, Woese proposed a new model to replace the standard Darwinian theory of common descent—that all life on Earth evolved from a single cell or pre-cell. Woese proposed instead that various forms of life evolved independently from as many as several dozen ancestral pre-cells. A 2004 paper further postulated that Darwinian natural selection did not become a factor in evolution until more complex life-forms evolved. Woese argued that in the early stages of the development of life, all organisms engaged in horizontal gene transfer and were not in competition.

rules about bacterial composition or structure, and there are many exceptions to any general statement.

Individual bacteria can assume one of three basic shapes: spherical (coccus), rodlike (bacillus), or curved (vibrio, spirillum, or spirochete). Considerable variation is seen in the actual shapes of bacteria, and cells can be stretched or compressed in one dimension. Bacteria that do not separate from one another after cell division form characteristic clus-

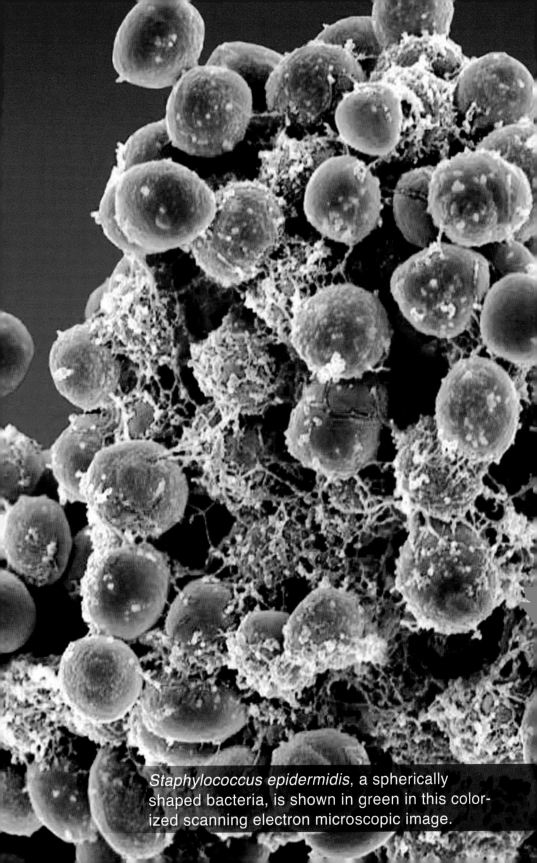

Staphylococcus epidermidis, a spherically shaped bacteria, is shown in green in this color-ized scanning electron microscopic image.

ters that are helpful in their identification. For example, some cocci are found mainly in pairs, including *Streptococcus pneumoniae*, a pneumococcus that causes bacterial lobar pneumonia, and *Neisseria gonorrhoeae*, a gonococcus that causes the sexually transmitted disease gonorrhea. Most streptococci resemble a long strand of beads, whereas the staphylococci form random clumps (the name "staphylococci" is derived from the Greek word *staphyle*, meaning "cluster of grapes"). In addition, some coccal bacteria occur as square or cubical packets. The rod-shaped bacilli usually occur singly, but some strains form long chains, such as rods of the corynebacteria, normal inhabitants of the mouth that are frequently attached to one another at random angles. Some bacilli have pointed ends, whereas others have squared ends, and some rods are bent into a comma shape. These bent rods are often called vibrios and include *Vibrio cholerae*, which causes cholera. Other shapes of bacteria include the spirilla, which are bent and rebent, and the spirochetes, which form a helix similar to a corkscrew, in which the cell body is wrapped around a central fibre called the axial filament.

Bacteria are the smallest living creatures. An average-size bacterium, such as the rod-shaped *Escherichia coli*, a normal inhabitant of the intestinal tract of humans and animals, is about 2 micrometres (μm; millionths of a metre) long and 0.5 μm in diameter, and the spherical cells of *Staphylococcus aureus* are up to 1 μm in diameter. A few bacterial types are even smaller, such as *Mycoplasma pneumoniae*, which is one of the smallest bacteria, ranging from about 0.1 to 0.25 μm in diameter; the rod-shaped *Bordetella pertussis*, which is the causative agent of whooping cough, ranging from 0.2 to 0.5 μm in diameter and 0.5 to 1 μm in length; and the cork screw shaped *Treponema pallidum*, which is the causative agent of syphilis, averaging only 0.15 μm in diameter but 10 to 13 μm in length. Some bacteria are relatively large, such as *Azotobacter*, which has diameters of 2 to 5 μm or more; the cyanobacterium *Synechococcus*, which averages 6 μm by 12 μm; and Achromatium, which has a minimum width of 5 μm and a maximum length of 100 μm, depending on the species. Giant bacteria can be visible with the unaided eye, such as *Titanospirillum namibiensis*, which averages 750 μm in diameter, and the rod-shaped *Epulopiscium fishelsoni*, which averages 80 μm in diameter by 600 μm in length.

Bacteria are unicellular microorganisms and thus are generally not organized into tissues. Each bacterium grows and divides independently of any other bacterium, although aggregates of bacteria, sometimes containing members of different species, are frequently found. Many bacteria can form aggregated structures called biofilms. Organisms in biofilms often display substantially different properties from the same organism in the individual state or the planktonic state. Bacteria that have aggregated into biofilms can communicate information about population size and metabolic state.

CELLULAR FEATURES

Bacteria possess unique features of cellular form and structure that distinguish them not only from organisms in the other domains of life but also from one another. The biochemical and structural components of their cell walls are among the primary features used to classify bacteria. These features also play a role in determining their infectious properties. Bacteria are characterized further by the ability to secrete extracellular materials, by the presence of structures that enable motility or adherence to substrates, by the contents of their cytoplasm, and by the presence of cell-surface molecules that can be detected by specific antibodies. Antibody detection forms the basis of the ability of the human immune system to recognize and remove disease-causing bacteria from the body.

THE GRAM STAIN

Bacteria are so small that their presence was only first recognized in 1677, when the Dutch naturalist Leeuwenhoek saw microscopic organisms in a variety of substances with the aid of primitive micro-scopes (more similar in design to modern magni-fying glasses than modern microscopes), some of which were capable of more than 200-fold magni-fication. Now bacteria are usually examined under light microscopes capable of more than 1,000-fold magnification; however, details of their internal struc-ture can be observed only with the aid of much more powerful transmission electron microscopes. Unless special phase-contrast microscopes are used, bac-

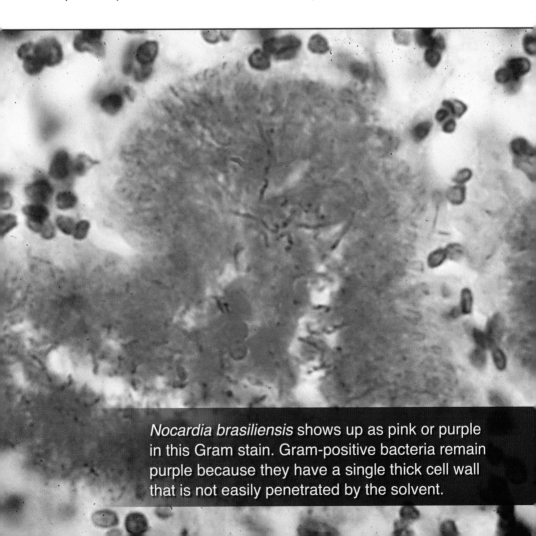

Nocardia brasiliensis shows up as pink or purple in this Gram stain. Gram-positive bacteria remain purple because they have a single thick cell wall that is not easily penetrated by the solvent.

teria have to be stained with a coloured dye so that they will stand out from their background.

One of the most useful staining reactions for bacteria is called the Gram stain, developed in 1884 by the Danish physician Hans Christian Gram. Bacteria in suspension are fixed to a glass slide by brief heating and then exposed to two dyes that combine to form a large blue dye complex within each cell. When the slide is flushed with an alcohol solution, Gram-positive bacteria retain the blue colour and Gram-negative bacteria lose the blue colour. The slide is then stained with a weaker pink dye that causes the Gram-negative bacteria to become pink, whereas the Gram-positive bacteria remain blue. The Gram stain reacts to differences in the structure of the bacterial cell surface, differences that are apparent when the cells are viewed under an electron microscope.

THE CELL ENVELOPE

The bacterial cell surface (or envelope) can vary considerably in its structure, and it plays a central role in the properties and capabilities of the cell. The one feature present in all cells is the cytoplasmic membrane, which separates the inside of the cell from its external environment, regulates the flow of nutrients, maintains the proper intracellular milieu, and prevents the loss of the cell's contents. The cytoplasmic membrane carries out many necessary cellular functions, including energy generation, protein secretion, chromosome segregation, and efficient active transport of nutrients. It is a typical unit membrane composed of proteins and lipids, basically similar to the membrane that surrounds all eukaryotic cells. It appears in electron micrographs as a triple-layered structure of lipids and proteins that completely surround the cytoplasm.

Lying outside of this membrane is a rigid wall that determines the shape of the bacterial cell. The wall is made of a huge molecule called peptidoglycan (or murein). In Gram-positive bacteria the peptidoglycan forms a thick mesh-like layer that retains the blue dye of the Gram stain by trapping it in the cell. In contrast, in Gram-negative bacteria the peptidoglycan layer is very thin (only one or two molecules deep), and the blue dye is easily washed out of the cell.

Peptidoglycan occurs only in the Bacteria (except for those without a cell wall, such as *Mycoplasma*). Peptidoglycan is a long-chain polymer of two repeating sugars (n-acetylglucosamine and n-acetylmuramic acid), in which adjacent sugar chains are linked to one another by peptide bridges that confer rigid stability. The nature of the peptide bridges differs considerably between species of bacteria but in general consists of four amino acids: L-alanine linked to D-glutamic acid, linked to either diaminopimelic acid in Gram-negative bacteria or L-lysine, L-ornithine, or diaminopimelic acid in Gram-positive bacteria, which is finally linked to D-alanine. In Gram-negative bacteria the peptide bridges connect the D-alanine on one chain to the diaminopimelic acid on another chain. In Gram-positive bacteria there can be an additional peptide chain that extends the reach of the cross-link; for example, there is an additional bridge of five glycines in *Staphylococcus aureus.*

Peptidoglycan synthesis is the target of many useful antimicrobial agents, including the β-lactam antibiotics (e.g., penicillin) that block the cross-linking of the peptide bridges. Some of the proteins that animals synthesize as natural antibacterial defense factors attack the cell walls of bacteria. For example, an enzyme called lysozyme splits the sugar chains that are the backbone of peptidoglycan molecules. The action of any of these agents weakens the cell wall and disrupts the bacterium.

In Gram-positive bacteria the cell wall is composed mainly of a thick peptidoglycan meshwork interwoven with other polymers called teichoic acids (from the Greek word *teichos*, meaning "wall") and some proteins or lipids. In contrast, Gram-negative bacteria have a complex cell wall that is composed of multiple layers in which an outer membrane layer lies on top of a thin peptidoglycan layer. This outer membrane is composed of phospholipids, which are complex lipids that contain molecules of phosphate, and lipopolysaccharides, which are complex lipids that are anchored in the outer membrane of cells by their lipid end and have a long chain of sugars extending away from the cell into the medium. Lipopolysaccharides, often called endotoxins, are toxic to animals and humans; their presence in the bloodstream can cause fever, shock, and even death. For most Gram-negative bacteria, the outer membrane forms a barrier to the passage of many chemicals that would be harmful to the bacterium, such as dyes and detergents that normally dissolve cellular membranes. Impermeability to oil-soluble compounds is not seen in other biological membranes and results from the presence of lipopolysaccharides in the membrane and from the unusual character of the outer membrane proteins. As evidence of the ability of the outer membrane to confer resistance to harsh environmental conditions, some Gram-negative bacteria grow well in oil slicks, jet fuel tanks, acid mine drainage, and even bottles of disinfectants.

The Archaea have markedly different surface structures from the Bacteria. They do not have peptidoglycan; instead, their membrane lipids are made up of branched isoprenoids linked to glycerol by ether bonds. Some archaea have a wall material that is similar to peptidoglycan, except that the specific sugar linked to the amino acid bridges is not muramic acid but talosaminuronic acid. Many other archaeal species use proteins as the basic constituent of their walls, and some lack a rigid wall.

CAPSULES AND SLIME LAYERS

Many bacterial cells secrete some extracellular material in the form of a capsule or a slime layer. A slime layer is loosely associated with the bacterium and can be easily washed off, whereas a capsule is attached tightly to the bacterium and has definite boundaries. Capsules can be seen under a light microscope by placing the cells in a suspension of India ink. The capsules exclude the ink and appear as clear halos surrounding the bacterial cells. Capsules are usually polymers of simple sugars (polysaccharides), although the capsule of *Bacillus anthracis* is made of polyglutamic acid. Most capsules are hydrophilic ("water-loving") and may help the bacterium avoid desiccation (dehydration) by preventing water loss. Capsules can protect a bacterial cell from ingestion and destruction by white blood cells (phagocytosis). While the exact mechanism for escaping phagocytosis is unclear, it may occur because capsules make bacterial surface components more slippery, helping the bacterium to escape engulfment by phagocytic cells. The presence of a capsule in *Streptococcus pneumoniae* is the most important factor in its ability to cause pneumonia. Mutant strains of *S. pneumoniae* that have lost the ability to form a capsule are readily taken up by white blood cells and do not cause disease. The association of virulence and capsule formation is also found in many other species of bacteria.

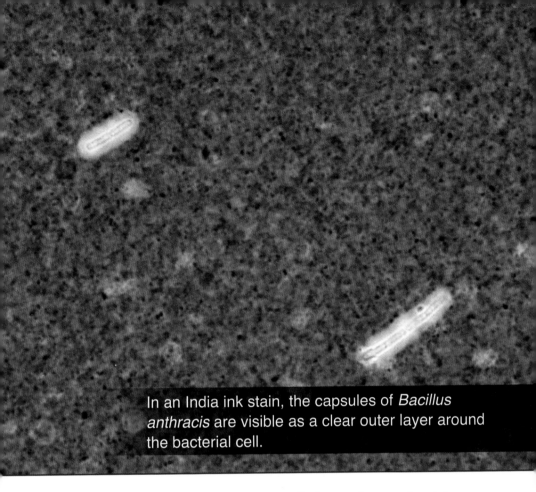

In an India ink stain, the capsules of *Bacillus anthracis* are visible as a clear outer layer around the bacterial cell.

A capsular layer of extracellular polysaccharide material can enclose many bacteria into a biofilm and serves many functions. *Streptococcus mutans*, which causes dental caries, splits the sucrose in food and uses one of the sugars to build its capsule, which sticks tightly to the tooth. The bacteria that are trapped in the capsule use the other sugar to fuel their metabolism and produce a strong acid (lactic acid) that attacks the tooth enamel. When *Pseudomonas aeruginosa* colonizes the lungs of persons with cystic fibrosis, it produces a thick capsular polymer of alginic acid that contributes to the difficulty of eradicating the bacterium. Bacteria of the genus *Zoogloea* secrete fibres of cellulose that enmesh the bacteria into a floc that floats on the surface of liquid and keeps the bacteria exposed to air, a requirement for the metabolism of this genus. A few rod-shaped bacteria, such as *Sphaerotilus*, secrete long chemically complex tubular sheaths that enclose substantial numbers of the bacteria. The sheaths of these and many other environmental bacteria can become encrusted with iron or manganese oxides.

FLAGELLA, FIMBRIAE, AND PILI

Many bacteria are motile, able to swim through a liquid medium or glide or swarm across a solid surface. Swimming and swarming bacteria possess flagella, which are the extracellular appendages needed for motility.

Flagella are long, helical filaments made of a single type of protein called flagellin and located either at the ends of rod-shaped cells, as in *Vibrio cholerae* or *Pseudomonas aeruginosa*, or all over the cell surface, as in *Escherichia coli*. Flagella can be found on both Gram-positive and Gram-negative rods but are rare on cocci and are trapped in the axial filament in the spirochetes. The flagellum is attached at its base to a basal body in the cell membrane. The protomotive force generated at the membrane is used to turn the flagellar filament, in the manner of a turbine driven by the flow of hydrogen ions through the basal body into the cell. When the flagella are rotating in a counterclockwise direction, the bacterial cell swims in a straight line; clockwise rotation results in swimming in the opposite direction or, if there is more than one flagellum per cell, in random tumbling. Chemotaxis allows a bacterium to adjust its swimming behaviour so that it can sense and migrate toward increasing levels of an attractant chemical or away from a repellent one.

Not only are bacteria able to swim or glide toward more favourable environments, but they also have appendages that allow them to adhere to surfaces and keep from being washed away by flowing fluids. Some bacteria produce straight, rigid, spike-like projections called fimbriae (Latin for "threads" or "fibres") or pili (Latin for "hairs"), which extend from the surface of the bacterium and attach to specific sugars on other cells. For example, *E. coli* bacteria possess pili that enable them to adhere to intestinal and urinary-tract epithelial cells. Likewise, the pili of *Neisseria gonorrhoeae* facilitate the organisms' attachment to epithelial cells lining the urinary tract. Fimbriae are present only in Gram-negative bacteria. Certain pili (called sex pili) are used to allow one bacterium to recognize and adhere to another in a process of sexual mating called conjugation. Many aquatic bacteria produce an acidic mucopolysaccharide holdfast, which allows them to adhere tightly to rocks or other surfaces.

CYTOPLASM

Although bacteria differ substantially in their surface structures, their interior contents are quite similar and display relatively few structural features. Indeed, all bacterial cells are filled with a semifluid substance known as cytoplasm. Within the cytoplasm, however, lies the bacterium's genetic material, the code that ultimately determines the uniqueness of every type of bacteria. The components necessary for the translation of the genetic material into proteins, as well as various storage vessels, are also found in the cytoplasm.

The genetic information of all cells resides in the sequence of nitrogenous bases in the extremely long molecules of DNA. Unlike the DNA in eukaryotic cells, which resides in the nucleus, DNA in bacterial cells is not sequestered in a membrane-bound organelle but appears as a long coil distributed through the cytoplasm. In many bacteria the DNA is present as a single, circular chromosome, although some bacteria may contain two chromosomes, and in some cases the DNA is linear rather than circular. A variable number of smaller, usually circular DNA molecules, called plasmids, can carry auxiliary information.

The sequence of bases in the DNA has been determined for hundreds of bacteria. The amount of DNA in bacterial chromosomes ranges from 580,000 base pairs in *Mycoplasma gallinarum* to 4,700,000 base pairs in *E. coli* to 9,140,000 base pairs in *Myxococcus xanthus*. The length of the *E. coli* chromosome is about 1.2 mm, which is striking in view of the fact that the length of the cell is about 0.001 mm.

As in all organisms, bacterial DNA contains the four nitrogenous bases adenine (A), cytosine (C), guanine (G), and thymine (T). The rules of base pairing for double-stranded DNA molecules require that the number of adenine and thymine bases be equal and that the number of cytosine and guanine bases also be equal. The relationship between the number of pairs of G and C bases and the number of pairs of A and T bases is an important indicator of evolutionary and adaptive genetic changes within an organism. The proportion, or molar ratio, of G + C can be measured as G + C divided by the sum of all the bases (A + T + G + C) multiplied by 100 percent. The extent to which G + C ratios vary between organisms may be considerable. In plants and animals, the proportion of G + C is about 50 percent. A far wider range in the proportion of G + C is seen in prokaryotes, extending from about 25 percent in most *Mycoplasma* to about 50 percent in *E. coli* to nearly 75 percent in *Micrococcus*, actinomycetes, and fruiting myxobacteria. The G + C content within a species in a single genus, however, is very similar.

The cytoplasm of bacteria contains high concentrations of enzymes, metabolites, and salts. In addition, the proteins of the cell are made on ribosomes that are scattered throughout the cytoplasm. Ribosomes are tiny particles that are present in large numbers in all living cells and serve as the site of protein synthesis. Bacterial ribosomes are different from ribosomes in eukaryotic cells in that they are smaller, have fewer constituents (consist of three types of ribosomal RNA [rRNA and 55 proteins, as opposed to four types of rRNA and 78 proteins in eukaryotes), and are inhibited by antibiotics.

There are numerous inclusion bodies, or granules, in the bacterial cytoplasm. These bodies are never enclosed by a membrane and serve as storage vessels. Glycogen, which is a polymer of glucose, is stored as a reserve of carbohydrate and energy. Volutin, or metachromatic granules, contains polymerized phosphate and represents a storage form for inorganic phosphate and energy. Many bacteria possess lipid droplets that contain polymeric esters of poly-β-hydroxybutyric acid or related compounds. This is in contrast to eukaryotes, which use lipid droplets to store triglycerides. In bacteria, storage granules are produced under favourable growth conditions and are consumed after the nutrients have been depleted from the medium. Many aquatic bacteria produce gas vacuoles, which are protein-bound structures that contain air and allow the bacteria to adjust their buoyancy. Bacteria can also have internal membranous structures that form as outgrowths of the cytoplasmic membrane.

BIOTYPES

The fact that pathogenic bacteria are constantly battling their host's immune system might account for the bewildering number of different strains, or types, of bacteria that belong to the same species but are distinguishable by serological tests. Microbiologists often identify bacteria by the presence of specific molecules on their cell surfaces, which are detected with specific antibodies. Antibodies are serum proteins that bind very tightly to foreign molecules (antigens) in an immune reaction aimed at removing or destroying the antigens. Antibodies have remarkable specificity, and the substitution of even one amino acid in a protein might prevent that protein from being recognized by an antibody.

In the case of *E. coli* and *Salmonella enterica*, there are thousands of different strains (called serovars, for serological variants), which differ from one another mainly or solely in the antigenic identity of their lipopolysaccharide, flagella, or capsule. Different serovars of these enteric bacteria are often found to be associated with the ability to inhabit different host animals or to cause different diseases. Formation of these numerous serovars reflects the ability of bacteria to respond effectively to the intense defensive actions of the immune system.

REPRODUCTION

Bacteria can reproduce in various ways. The most basic process is known as binary fission, which is characterized by bacterial cell growth and DNA replication that results in the splitting of one cell into two cells. This mode of reproduction produces two daughter cells that are identical to that of the parent cell. Binary fission alone, however, provides little benefit in the way of maintaining genetic diversity, which is important for the long-term success and evolution of species of bacteria.

In most animals and in certain plants, genetic variation within a species is frequently the result of sexual reproduction, in which the recombination of genes from two parent organisms produces a genetically distinct offspring. In the absence of sexual reproduction, bacteria have evolved multiple methods to secure opportunities for genetic recombination, both within and between species. This enables the organisms to incorporate new genes into their genomes. However, while genetic exchange drives the perpetual evolution of bacteria, allowing the organisms to adapt in response to new conditions, it also underlies the phenomenon of antibiotic resistance, which has become a significant concern in the medical treatment of bacterial infection.

REPRODUCTIVE PROCESSES

Asexual reproduction, in the form of binary fission, budding, or sporulation, represents the primary mode of reproduction utilized by bacteria. Asexual reproduction is augmented by genetic exchange, which occurs via three different mechanisms: transformation, transduction, or conjugation. In these processes, bacteria may take up genetic material freely (transformation), may receive genetic material from a special type of bacteria-infecting virus (transduction), or may temporarily combine physically with other bacterial cells to swap genes (conjugation).

BINARY FISSION

Most prokaryotes reproduce by a process of binary fission, in which the cell grows in volume until it divides in half to yield two identical daughter cells. Each daughter cell can continue to grow at the same rate as its parent. For this process to occur, the cell must grow over its entire surface until the time of cell division, when a new hemispherical pole forms at the division septum in the middle of the cell. In Gram-positive bacteria the septum grows inward from the plasma membrane along the midpoint of the cell; in Gram-negative bacteria the walls are more flexible, and the division septum forms as the side walls pinch inward, dividing the cell in two. In order for the cell to divide in half, the peptidoglycan structure must be different in the hemispherical cap than in the straight portion of the cell wall, and different wall cross-linking enzymes must be active at the septum than elsewhere.

BUDDING

A group of environmental bacteria reproduces by budding. In this process a small bud forms at one end of the mother cell or on filaments called prosthecae. As growth proceeds, the size of the mother cell remains about constant, but the bud enlarges. When the bud is about the same size as the mother cell, it separates. This type of reproduction is analogous to that in budding fungi, such as brewer's yeast (*Saccharomyces cerevisiae*). One difference between fission and budding is that, in the latter, the mother cell often has different properties from the offspring. In some *Pasteuria* strains, the daughter buds have a flagellum and are motile, whereas the mother cells lack flagella but have long pili and holdfast appendages at the end opposite the bud. The related *Planctomyces*, found in plankton, have long fibrillar stalks at the end opposite the bud. In *Hyphomicrobium* a hyphal filament (prostheca) grows out of one end of

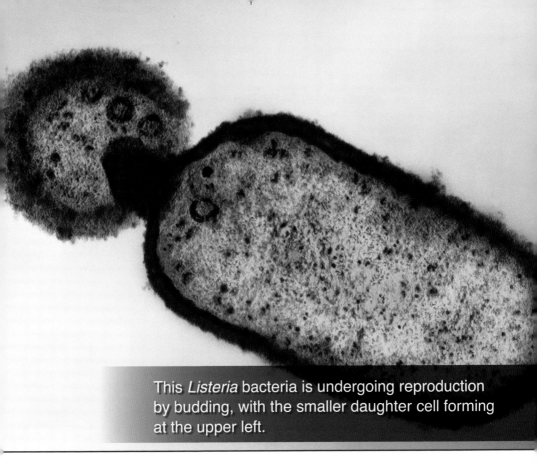

This *Listeria* bacteria is undergoing reproduction by budding, with the smaller daughter cell forming at the upper left.

the cell, and the bud grows out of the tip of the prostheca, separated by a relatively long distance from the mother cell.

SPORULATION

Many environmental bacteria are able to produce stable dormant, or resting, forms as a branch of their life cycle to enhance their survival under adverse conditions. These processes are not an obligate stage of the cell's life cycle but rather an interruption. Such dormant forms are called endospores, cysts, or heterocysts (primarily seen in cyanobacteria), depending on the method of spore formation, which differs between groups of bacteria.

The ability to form endospores is found among bacteria in a number of genera, predominantly Gram-positive groups, including the aerobic rod *Bacillus*, the microaerophilic rod *Sporolactobacillus*, the anaerobic rods *Clostridium* and *Desulfotomaculum*, the coccus *Sporosarcina*, and the filamentous *Thermoactinomyces*. The formation of a spore occurs in response to nutritional deprivation. Consequently, endospores do not possess metabolic activity until nutrients become available, at which time they are able to differentiate from spores into vegetative cells. Only one spore is formed inside each bacterial cell during sporulation. The formation of a spore begins with invagination of the cytoplasmic membrane around a copy of the bacterial chromosome, thus separating the contents of the smaller cell from the mother cell. The membrane of the mother cell engulfs the smaller cell within its cytoplasm, effectively providing two concentric unit membranes to protect the developing spore. A thin spore membrane and a thick cortex of a peptidoglycan are laid down between the two unit membranes. A rigid spore coat forms outside the cortex, enclosing the entire spore structure. The spore coat has keratin-like properties that are able to resist the lethal effects of heat, desiccation (dehydration), freezing, chemicals, and radiation. The ability of endospores to resist these noxious agents may ensue from the extremely low water content inside the spore. Methane-oxidizing bacteria in the genus *Methylosinus* also produce desiccation-resistant spores, called exospores.

Cysts are thick-walled structures produced by dormant members of *Azotobacter, Bdellovibrio* (bdellocysts), and *Myxococcus* (myxospores). They are resistant to desiccation and other harmful conditions but to a lesser degree than are endospores. In encystment by the nitrogen-fixing *Azotobacter,* cell division is followed by the formation of a thick, multilayered wall and coat that surround the resting cell. The filamentous actinomycetes produce reproductive spores of two categories: conidiospores, which are chains of multiple spores formed on aerial or substrate mycelia, or sporangiospores, which are formed in specialized sacs called sporangia.

EXCHANGE OF GENETIC INFORMATION

Bacteria do not have an obligate sexual reproductive stage in their life cycle, but they can be very active in the exchange of genetic information. The genetic information carried in the DNA can be transferred from one cell to another; however, this is not a true exchange, because only one partner receives the new information. In addition, the amount of DNA that is transferred is usually only a small piece of the chromosome. There are several mechanisms by which this takes place. In transformation, bacteria take up free fragments of DNA that are floating in the medium. To take up the DNA efficiently, bacterial cells must be in a competent state, which is defined by the capability of bacteria to bind free fragments of DNA and is formed naturally only in a limited number of bacteria, such as *Haemophilus*, *Neisseria*, *Streptococcus*, and *Bacillus*. Many other bacteria, including *E. coli*, can be rendered competent artificially under laboratory conditions, such as by exposure to solutions of calcium chloride ($CaCl_2$). Transformation is a major tool in recombinant DNA technology, because fragments of DNA from one organism can be taken up by a second organism, thus allowing the second organism to acquire new characteristics.

Transduction is the transfer of DNA from one bacterium to another by means of a bacteria-infecting virus called a bacteriophage. Transduction is an efficient means of transferring DNA between bacteria because DNA enclosed in the bacteriophage is protected from physical decay and from attack by enzymes in the environment and is injected directly into cells by the bacteriophage. However, widespread gene transfer by means of transduction is of limited significance because the packaging of bacterial DNA into a virus is inefficient and the bacteriophages are usually highly restricted in the range of bacterial species that they can infect. Thus, interspecies transfer of DNA by transduction is rare.

Conjugation is the transfer of DNA by direct cell-to-cell contact that is mediated by plasmids (nonchromosomal DNA molecules). Conjugative plasmids encode an extremely efficient mechanism that mediates their own transfer from a donor cell to a recipient cell. The process takes place in one direction since only the donor cells contain the conjugative plasmid. In Gram-negative bacteria, donor cells produce a specific plasmid-coded pilus, called the sex pilus, which attaches the donor cell to the recipient cell. Once connected, the two cells are brought into direct contact, and a conjugal bridge forms through which the DNA is transferred from the donor to the recipient.

Many conjugative plasmids can be transferred between, and reproduce in, a large number of different Gram-negative bacterial species. Some chemolithotrophic bacteria (bacteria that derive energy from inorganic compounds) carry plasmids that are very large, ranging in size from 400,000 to 700,000 base pairs. Although plasmids are not essential for the bacterium, they may confer a selective advantage. One class of plasmids, colicinogenic (or *Col*) factors, determines the production of proteins called colicins, which have antibiotic activity and can kill other bacteria. Another class of plasmids, R factors, confers upon bacteria resistance to antibiotics. Some *Col* factors and R factors can transfer themselves from one cell to another and thus are capable of spreading rapidly through a bacterial population. A plasmid that is attached to the cell membrane or integrated into the bacterial chromosome is called an episome.

Episomes represent a specialized group of plasmids. They may be attached to the bacterial cell membrane (such a cell is designated F^+) or become integrated into the chromosome (such a cell is designated Hfr). F^+ and Hfr cells act as donors during conjugation. Cells lacking the episome (called F^- cells) may receive either the episome (from an F^+ cell) or the episome plus the chromosomal genes to which it is attached (from an Hfr cell). Some bacterial viruses, called temperate phages, carry DNA that can act as an episome. A bacterial cell into whose chromosome the viral DNA has become integrated is called a prophage.

The bacterial chromosome can also be transferred during conjugation, although this happens less frequently than plasmid transfer. Conjugation allows the inheritance of large portions of genes and may be responsible for the existence of bacteria with traits of several different species. Conjugation also has been observed in the Gram-positive genus *Enterococcus*, but the mechanism of cell recognition and DNA transfer is different from that which occurs in Gram-negative bacteria.

In addition to the important role plasmids fulfill naturally in bacteria, they are also extremely valuable tools in the fields of molecular biology and genetics, specifically in the area of genetic engineering. They play a critical role in such procedures as gene cloning, recombinant protein production (e.g., of human insulin), and gene therapy research. In such procedures, a plasmid is cut at a specific site (or sites) using enzymes called restriction endonucleases. A foreign DNA element (such as the gene for insulin) is then spliced into the plasmid. The resulting circular structure, a recombinant DNA molecule, is then introduced into bacterial cells via transformation. The autonomous replication of the plasmid within the bacterial cells makes it possible to produce large numbers of copies of the recombinant DNA molecule for experimental manipulation or commercial purposes (such as the production of large amounts of insulin). Plasmids are well suited to genetic engineering in other ways. Their antibiotic resistance genes, for example, prove useful in identifying those bacterial cells that have taken up the recombinant DNA molecule in a high background of untransformed cells (transformation frequencies are only about 1 out of every 100,000 cells).

GROWTH, IMPORTANCE, AND EVOLUTION OF BACTERIA

T
he ability of bacteria to thrive in specific habitats, such as the human intestine or forest soil, is a function of both nutritional and physical factors. Each type of bacteria has specific growth requirements, which may be decided by an organism's ability to metabolize only one kind of carbohydrate or to tolerate only certain pH levels and temperatures. Thus, the relationship between bacteria and the environment, as well as between bacteria and plants, animals, and other organisms, is a reflection of their specific growth requirements. These specifications are in turn the product of millions of years of evolution and adaptation.

GROWTH OF BACTERIAL POPULATIONS

The growth of bacterial populations is dependent on both the extent of nutrients available in a given environment and the various growth requirements of the organisms. Bacterial growth rates are highly variable. Division cycles and population doubling for some species may take only minutes, whereas for others these processes may take days. Growth rates and the limitations imposed by nutrient availability and metabolic requirements have been studied extensively in the laboratory. As a result, there exists a large body of knowledge concerning the various metabolic pathways utilized by different organisms, which has enabled microbiologists to calculate and predict the generation times for specific types of bacteria under all sorts of growth conditions.

Growth of bacterial cultures is defined as an increase in the number of bacteria in a population rather than in the size of individual cells. The growth of a bacterial population occurs in a geometric or exponential manner: with each division cycle (generation), one cell gives rise to 2 cells, then 4 cells, then 8 cells, then 16, then 32, and so forth. The time required for the formation of a generation, the generation time (G), can be calculated from the following formula:

$$G = \frac{t}{n} = \frac{t}{3.3 \log b/B}.$$

In the formula, B is the number of bacteria present at the start of the observation, b is the number present after the time period t, and n is the number of generations. The relationship shows that the mean generation time is constant and that the rate at which the number of bacteria increases is proportional to the number of bacteria at any given time. This relationship is valid only during the period when the population is increasing in an exponential manner, called the log phase of growth. For this reason, graphs that show the growth of bacterial cultures are plotted as the logarithm of the number of cells.

The generation time, which varies among bacteria, is controlled by many environmental conditions and by the nature of the bacterial species. For example, *Clostridium perfringens*, one of the fastest-growing bacteria, has an optimum generation time of about 10 minutes; *Escherichia coli* can double every 20 minutes; and the slow-growing *Mycobacterium tuberculosis* has a generation time in the range of 12 to 16 hours. The composition of the growth medium is a major factor controlling the growth rate. The growth rate increases up to a maximum when the medium provides a better energy source and more of the biosynthetic intermediates that the cell would otherwise have to make for itself.

When bacteria are placed in a medium that provides all of the nutrients that are necessary for their growth, the population exhibits four phases of growth that are representative of a typical bacterial growth curve. Upon inoculation into the new medium, bacteria do not immediately reproduce, and the population size remains constant. During this

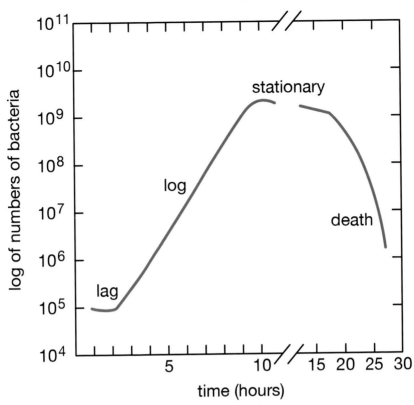

Generalized bacterial growth curve showing the phases in the growth of bacterial colonies.

period, called the lag phase, the cells are metabolically active and increase only in cell size. They are also synthesizing the enzymes and factors needed for cell division and population growth under their new environmental conditions. The population then enters the log phase, in which cell numbers increase in a logarithmic fashion, and each cell generation occurs in the same time interval as the preceding ones, resulting in a balanced increase in the constituents of each cell. The log phase continues until nutrients are depleted or toxic products accumulate, at which time the cell growth rate slows, and some cells may begin to die. Under optimum conditions, the maximum population for some bacterial species at the end of the log phase can reach a density of 10 to 30 billion cells per millilitre.

The log phase of bacterial growth is followed by the stationary phase, in which the size of a population of bacteria remains constant, even though some cells continue to divide and others begin to die. The stationary phase is followed by the death phase, in which the death of cells in the population exceeds the formation of new cells. The length of time before the onset of the death phase depends on the species and the medium.

Bacteria do not necessarily die even when starved of nutrients, and they can remain viable for long periods of time.

FACTORS AFFECTING BACTERIAL GROWTH

As a group, bacteria depend on a wide range of substances for their growth. In general, however, in order for any type of bacterial cell to grow, it requires a source of carbon and a source of energy. How bacterial cells utilize the substances in their environments to obtain carbon and energy varies substantially, and this underlies the diversity of metabolic pathways seen throughout the Bacteria domain. Thus, whereas the absence of a specific nutrient may not have any affect on the growth of one type of bacteria, it may entirely prevent the growth of a different type. Likewise, the presence or absence of oxygen, extremely acidic or basic pH, and hot or cold temperatures can influence the growth of bacterial populations by altering their ability to derive carbon and energy from their surroundings.

NUTRITIONAL REQUIREMENTS

Bacteria differ dramatically with respect to the conditions that are necessary for their optimal growth. In terms of nutritional needs, all cells require sources of carbon, nitrogen, sulfur, phosphorus, numerous inorganic salts (e.g., potassium, magnesium, sodium, calcium, and iron), and a large number of other elements called micronutrients (e.g., zinc, copper, manganese, selenium, tungsten, and molybdenum). Carbon is the element required in the greatest amount by bacteria since hydrogen and oxygen can be obtained from water, which is a prerequisite for bacterial growth. Also required is a source of energy to fuel the metabolism of the bacterium. One means of organizing bacteria is based on these fundamental nutritional needs: the carbon source and the energy source.

There are two sources a cell can use for carbon: inorganic compounds and organic compounds.

Organisms that use the inorganic compound carbon dioxide (CO_2) as their source of carbon are called autotrophs. Bacteria that require an organic source of carbon, such as sugars, proteins, fats, or amino acids, are called heterotrophs (or organotrophs). Many heterotrophs, such as *Escherichia coli* or *Pseudomonas aeruginosa*, synthesize all of their cellular constituents from simple sugars such as glucose because they possess the necessary biosynthetic pathways. Other heterotrophs have lost some of these biosynthetic pathways; in order to grow, they require that their environments contain particular amino acids, nitrogenous bases, or vitamins that are chemically intact.

In addition to carbon, bacteria need energy, which is almost always obtained by the transfer of an electron from an electron donor to an electron acceptor. There are three basic sources of energy: light, inorganic compounds, and organic compounds. Phototrophic bacteria use photosynthesis to generate cellular energy in the form of adenosine triphosphate (ATP) from light energy. Chemotrophs obtain their energy from chemicals (organic and inorganic compounds); chemolithotrophs obtain their energy from reactions with inorganic salts; and chemoheterotrophs obtain their carbon and energy from organic compounds (the energy source may also serve as the carbon source in these organisms).

In most cases, cellular energy is generated by means of electron-transfer reactions, in which electrons move from an organic or inorganic donor molecule to an acceptor molecule via a pathway that conserves the energy released during the transfer of electrons by trapping it in a form that the cell can use for its chemical or physical work. The primary form of energy that is captured from the transfer of electrons is ATP. The metabolic processes that break down organic molecules to generate energy are called catabolic reactions. In contrast, the metabolic processes that synthesize molecules are called anabolic reactions.

Many bacteria can use a large number of compounds as carbon and energy sources, whereas other bacteria are highly restricted in their metabolic capabilities. While carbohydrates are a common energy source for eukaryotes, these molecules are metabolized by only a limited number of species of bacteria, since most bacteria do not possess the necessary enzymes to metabolize these often complex molecules. Many species of bacteria instead depend on other energy sources, such as amino acids, fats, or other compounds. Other compounds of significance to bacteria include phosphate, sulfate, and nitrogen. Low levels of phosphate in many environments, particularly in water, can be a limiting factor for the growth of bacteria, since many bacteria cannot synthesize phosphate. Most bacteria can convert sulfate or sulfide to the organic form needed for protein synthesis. The capability of a living organism to incorporate nitrogen from ammonia is widespread in nature, and bacteria differ in their ability to convert other forms of nitrogen, such as nitrate in the soil or dinitrogen gas (N_2) in the atmosphere, into cell material.

A particularly important nutrient of bacteria is iron, an abundant element in the Earth's crust. Iron is a component of heme proteins, such as hemoglobin in red blood cells and cytochromes in electron transfer chains, as well as many other iron-containing proteins involved in electrontransfer reactions. Iron is needed for the growth of almost all organisms. In aerobic environments at neutral pH values, ferrous iron (iron in the +2 state) is oxidized to ferric iron (iron in the +3 state), which is virtually insoluble in water and unable to enter cells. Many bacteria synthesize and secrete chemicals called siderophores that bind very tightly to iron and make it soluble in water. The bacteria then take up these iron-siderophore complexes and remove the iron for their synthetic tasks. The ability to acquire iron in this way is particularly important to pathogenic (disease-causing) bacteria, which must compete with their host for iron. In anaerobic environments, iron can exist in the more soluble ferrous state and is readily available to bacteria.

Some bacteria are obligate parasites and grow only within a living host cell. *Rickettsia* and *Chla-*

mydia, for example, grow in eukaryotic cells, and *Bdellovibrio* grow in bacterial cells. *Treponema pallidum* is difficult, if not impossible, to grow in culture, probably because it requires low oxygen tension and low oxidation-reduction levels, which are provided by the presence of animal cells, rather than any specific nutrient. Because some bacteria may thrive only as animal or plant parasites or only in a rich source of nutrients such as milk, they likely do not thrive as free bacteria in nature. Many bacteria from natural environments exist in a consortium with other bacteria and are difficult to isolate and culture separately from the other members of that partnership.

PHYSICAL REQUIREMENTS

The physical requirements that are optimal for bacterial growth vary dramatically for different bacterial types. As a group, bacteria display the widest variation of all organisms in their ability to inhabit different environments. Some of the most prominent factors are described in the following sections.

OXYGEN

One of the most prominent differences between bacteria is their requirement for, and response to, atmospheric oxygen (O_2). Whereas essentially all eukaryotic organisms require oxygen to thrive, many species of bacteria can grow under anaerobic conditions. Bacteria that require oxygen to grow are called obligate aerobic bacteria. In most cases, these bacteria require oxygen to grow because their methods of energy production and respiration depend on the transfer of electrons to oxygen, which is the final electron acceptor in the electron transport reaction. Obligate aerobes include *Bacillus subtilis*, *Pseudomonas aeruginosa*, *Mycobacterium tuberculosis*, and *Thiobacillus ferrooxidans*.

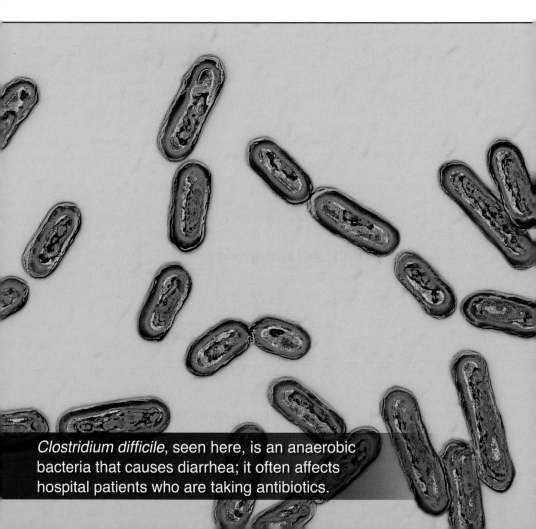

Clostridium difficile, seen here, is an anaerobic bacteria that causes diarrhea; it often affects hospital patients who are taking antibiotics.

Bacteria that grow only in the absence of oxygen, such as *Clostridium*, *Bacteroides*, and the methane-producing archaea (methanogens), are called obligate anaerobes because their energy-generating metabolic processes are not coupled with the consumption of oxygen. In fact, the presence of oxygen actually poisons some of their key enzymes. Some bacteria (*S. pneumoniae*) are microaerophilic or aerotolerant anaerobes because they grow better in low concentrations of oxygen. In these bacteria, oxygen often stimulates minor metabolic processes that enhance the major routes of energy production. Facultative anaerobes can change their metabolic processes depending on the presence of oxygen, using the more efficient process of respiration in the presence of oxygen and the less efficient process of fermentation in the absence of oxygen. Examples of facultative anaerobes include *E. coli* and *S. aureus*.

The response of bacteria to oxygen is not determined simply by their metabolic needs. Oxygen is a very reactive molecule and forms several toxic by-products such as superoxide (O_2^-), hydrogen peroxide (H_2O_2), and the hydroxyl radical ($OH \cdot$). Aerobic organisms produce enzymes that detoxify these oxygen products. The most common detoxifying enzymes are catalase, which breaks down hydrogen peroxide, and superoxide dismutase, which breaks down superoxide. The combined action of these enzymes to remove hydrogen peroxide and superoxide is important because these by-products together with iron form the extremely reactive hydroxyl radical, which is capable of killing the cell. Anaerobic bacteria generally do not produce catalase, and their levels of superoxide dismutase vary in rough proportion with the cell's sensitivity to oxygen. Many anaerobes are hypersensitive to oxygen, being killed upon short exposure, whereas other anaerobes, including most *Clostridium* species, are more tolerant to the presence of oxygen.

TEMPERATURE

Bacteria have adapted to a wide range of temperatures. Bacteria that grow at temperatures of less than about 15 °C (59 °F) are psychrophiles. The ability of bacteria to grow at low temperatures is not unexpected, since the average subsurface temperature of soil in the temperate zone is about 12 °C (54 °F) and 90 percent of the oceans measure 5 °C (41 °F) or colder. Obligate psychrophiles, which have been isolated from Arctic and Antarctic ocean waters and sediments, have optimum growth temperatures of about 10 °C (50 °F) and do not survive if exposed to 20°C (68 °F). The majority of psychrophilic bacteria are in the Gram-negative genera Pseudomonas, *Flavobacterium, Achromobacter,* and *Alcaligenes.* Mesophilic bacteria are those in which optimum growth occurs between 20 and 45 °C (68 and 113

°F), although they usually can survive and grow in temperatures between 10 and 50 °C (50 and 122 °F). Animal pathogens are mesophiles.

Thermophilic prokaryotes can grow at temperatures higher than 60 °C (140 °F). These temperatures are encountered in rotting compost piles, hot springs, and oceanic geothermal vents. In the runoff of a hot spring, thermophiles such as the bacterium *Thermus aquaticus* (optimum temperature for growth, 70 °C [158 °F]; maximum temperature, 79 °C [174 °F]) are found near the source where the temperature has fallen to about 70 °C. Thick mats of the cyanobacterium *Synechococcus* and the phototrophic gliding bacterium *Chloroflexus* develop in somewhat cooler portions of the runoff. The archaeon *Sulfolobus acidocaldarius* has a high tolerance for acidic conditions, which allows growth in a pH range of about 1.0 to 6.0 and a temperature optimum of 70 to 75 °C (158 to 167 °F). Numerous bacteria and archaea are adapted to the temperature range of 50 to 70 °C (122 to 158 °F), including some members of the genera *Bacillus*, *Thermoactinomyces*, *Methanobacterium*, *Methylococcus*, and *Sulfolobus*. Most striking was the discovery in the mid-1980s of bacteria and archaea in nutrient-rich, extremely hot hydrothermal vents on the deep seafloor. The archaea in the genus *Pyrodictium* thrive in the temperature range of 80 to 110 °C (176 to 230 °F), temperatures at which the water remains liquid only because of the extremely high pressures.

pH

Most bacteria grow in the range of neutral pH values (between 5 and 8), although some species have adapted to life at more acidic or alkaline extremes. An example of an acidophilic bacterium is *T. ferrooxidans*. When coal seams are exposed to air through mining operations, the pyritic ferrous sulfide deposits are attacked by *T. ferrooxidans* to generate sulfuric acid, which lowers the pH to 2.0 or even 0.7. However, acid tolerance of *T. ferrooxidans* applies only to sulfuric acid, since these bacteria die when exposed to equivalent concentrations of other acids such as hydrochloric acid. Many bacteria cannot tolerate acidic environments, especially under anaerobic conditions, and, as a result, plant polymers degrade slowly in acidic (pH between 3.7 and 5.5) bogs, pine forests, and lakes. In contrast to acidophilic bacteria, alkalophilic bacteria are able to grow in alkaline concentrations as great as pH 10 to 11. Alkalophiles have been isolated from soils, and most are species of the Gram-positive genus *Bacillus*.

SALT AND WATER

Water is a fundamental requirement for life. Some bacteria prefer salty environments and are thus called halophiles. Extreme halophiles, such as *Halobacterium*, show optimum growth in conditions of

20 to 30 percent salt and will lyse (break open) if this salt level is reduced. Such bacteria are found in the Dead Sea, in brine ponds, and occasionally on salted fishes and hides. Moderately halophilic bacteria grow in conditions of 5 to 20 percent salt and are found in salt brines and muds.

BACTERIAL METABOLISM

Heterotrophic, autotrophic, and phototrophic metabolism are three ways in which bacteria generate carbon and energy to support their growth. Whereas heterotrophs are dependent on organic compounds as sources for carbon and energy, autotrophs are dependent largely on carbon dioxide and inorganic substances. Phototrophs contain special pigment molecules that are able to derive energy from sunlight.

HETEROTROPHIC METABOLISM

Heterotrophic (or organotrophic) bacteria require organic molecules to provide their carbon and energy. The energy-yielding catabolic reactions can be of many different types, although they all involve electron-transfer reactions in which the movement of an electron from one molecule to another is coupled with an energy-trapping reaction that yields ATP. Some heterotrophic bacteria can metabolize sugars or complex carbohydrates to produce energy. These bacteria must produce a number of specific proteins, including enzymes that degrade the polysaccharides into their constituent sugar units, a transport system to accumulate the sugar inside the cell, and enzymes to convert the sugar into one of the central intermediates of metabolism, such as glucose-6-phosphate. There are several central pathways for carbohydrate utilization, including the Embden-Meyerhof pathway of glycolysis and the pentose phosphate pathway, both of which are also present in eukaryotic cells. Some bacteria possess the Entner-Doudoroff pathway, which converts glucose primarily to pyruvate, as well as other pathways that accomplish the conversion of glucose into smaller compounds with fewer enzyme-catalyzed steps.

Sugar metabolism produces energy for the cell via two different processes, fermentation and respiration. Fermentation is an anaerobic process that takes place in the absence of any external electron acceptor. The organic compound, such as a sugar or amino acid, is broken down into smaller organic molecules, which accept the electrons that had been released during the breakdown of the energy source. These catabolic reactions include a few steps that result in the direct formation of ATP. When glucose is broken down to lactic acid, as occurs in some *Streptococcus* and *Lactobacillus* species, as well as in muscle cells in higher eukaryotes, each molecule of glucose yields only two molecules of

ATP, and considerable quantities of glucose must be degraded to provide sufficient energy for bacterial growth. Because organic molecules are only partially oxidized during fermentation, the growth of fermentative bacteria results in the production of large quantities of organic end products and a relatively small output of energy per glucose molecule consumed. Few bacteria produce only lactic acid, which is fairly toxic for bacteria and limits the growth of a colony. A variety of additional fermentation pathways are used by specific bacteria to break down glucose; the characteristic end products of these pathways assist in the identification of the bacteria. These end products are often less toxic than lactic acid or are formed with the harnessing of additional metabolic energy. For example, the products of mixed-acid fermentation in *E. coli* include lactic acid, succinic acid, acetic acid, formic acid, ethyl alcohol, carbon dioxide, and hydrogen gas. *Enterobacter aerogenes* produces most of the same set of fermentation products, as well as large amounts of 2,3-butylene glycol, which is nonacidic and permits more bacterial growth.

Considerably more energy is available to the cell from respiration, a process in which the electrons from molecules of sugar are transferred not to another organic molecule but to an inorganic molecule. The most familiar respiratory process (aerobic respiration) uses oxygen as the final electron acceptor. The sugar is completely broken down to carbon dioxide and water, yielding a maximum of 38 molecules of ATP per molecule of glucose. Electrons are transferred to oxygen using the electron transport chain, a system of enzymes and cofactors located in the cell membrane and arranged so that the passage of electrons down the chain is coupled with the movement of protons (hydrogen ions) across the membrane and out of the cell. Electron transport induces the movement of positively charged hydrogen ions to the outside of the cell and negatively charged ions to its interior. This ion gradient results in the acidification of the external medium and an energized plasma membrane with an electrical charge of 150 to 200 millivolts. The generation of ion gradients, including this proton-motive force (gradient of protons), is a common aspect of energy generation and storage in all living organisms. The gradient of protons is used directly by the cell for many processes, including the active transport of nutrients and the rotation of flagella. The protons also can move from the exterior of the cell into the cytoplasm by passing through a membrane enzyme called the F_1F_0-proton-translocating ATPase, which couples this proton movement to ATP synthesis in a process identical to that which occurs in the mitochondria of eukaryotic cells. Bacteria that are able to use respiration produce far more energy per sugar molecule than do fermentative cells, because the complete oxidation (breakdown) of the energy source allows complete extraction of all of the energy available as shown by the substantially greater yield of ATP for respiring organisms than for fermenting bacteria. Respiring organisms achieve a greater yield of cell material using a given amount of nutrient; they also generate fewer toxic end products. The solubility of oxygen in water is limited, however, and the growth and survival of populations of aerobic bacteria are directly proportional to the available supply of oxygen. Continuous supplies of oxygen are available only to bacteria that come into contact with air, as occurs when bacteria are able to float on a surface that exposes them to air or when the medium in which the bacteria live is stirred vigorously.

Respiration can also occur under anaerobic conditions by processes called anaerobic respiration, in which the final electron acceptor is an inorganic molecule, such as nitrate (NO_3^-), nitrite (NO_2^-), sulfate (SO_4^{2-}), or carbon dioxide (CO_2). The energy yields available to the cell using these acceptors are lower than in respiration with oxygen—much lower in the case of sulfate and carbon dioxide—but they are still substantially higher than the energy yields available from fermentation. The ability of some bacteria to use inorganic molecules in anaerobic respiration can have environmental significance. *E. coli* can use oxygen, nitrate, or nitrite as an electron acceptor, and *Pseudomonas stutzeri* is of major global importance for its activity in denitrification, the conversion of nitrate to nitrite and dinitrogen gas (N_2). *Desulfovibrio* and *Desulfuromonas* reduce sulfate and elemental sulfur (S), respectively, yielding sulfide (S^{2-}), and the bacterium *Acetobacterium woodii* and methanogenic archaea, such as *Methanobacterium thermautotrophicum*, reduce carbon dioxide to acetate and methane, respectively. The Archaea typically use hydrogen as an electron donor with carbon dioxide as an electron acceptor to yield methane or with sulfate as an electron acceptor to yield sulfide.

AUTOTROPHIC METABOLISM

Autotrophic bacteria synthesize all their cell constituents using carbon dioxide as the carbon source. The most common pathways for synthesizing organic compounds from carbon dioxide are the reductive pentose phosphate (Calvin) cycle, the reductive tricarboxylic acid cycle, and the acetyl-CoA pathway. The Calvin cycle, elucidated by American biochemist Melvin Calvin, is the most widely distributed of these pathways, operating in plants, algae, photosynthetic bacteria, and most aerobic lithoautotrophic bacteria. The key step in the Calvin cycle is the reaction of ribulose 1,5-bisphosphate with carbon dioxide, yielding two molecules of 3-phosphoglycerate, a precursor to glucose. This cycle is extremely expensive for the cell in terms of energy, such that the synthesis of one molecule of glyceraldehyde-

3-phosphate requires the consumption of nine molecules of ATP and the oxidation of six molecules of the electron donor, the reduced form of nicotinamide adenine dinucleotide phosphate (NADPH). Autotrophic behaviour depends on the ability of the cell to carry out photosynthetic or aerobic respiratory metabolism, which are the only processes able to deliver sufficient energy to maintain carbon fixation.

The aerobic nonphotosynthetic lithoautotrophs are those bacteria that not only use carbon dioxide as their sole carbon source but also generate energy from inorganic compounds (electron donors) with oxygen as an electron acceptor. These bacteria are taxonomically diverse and are usually defined by the electron donor that they use. For example, *Nitrosomonas europaea* oxidizes ammonia (NH_4^+) to nitrite, and *Nitrobacter winogradsky* oxidizes nitrite to nitrate. *Thiobacillus* oxidizes thiosulfate and elemental sulfur to sulfate, and *T. ferrooxidans* oxidizes ferrous ions to the ferric form. This diverse oxidizing ability allows *T. ferrooxidans* to tolerate high concentrations of many different ions, including iron, copper, cobalt, nickel, and zinc. All of these types of bacteria appear to be obligate lithotrophs and are unable to use organic compounds to a significant degree. Carbon monoxide (CO) is oxidized to carbon dioxide by *Pseudomonas carboxydovorans*, and hydrogen gas (H_2) is oxidized by *Alcaligenes eutrophus* and, to a lesser degree, by many other bacteria.

Metabolic energy is made available from the oxidation of these electron donors in basically the same way as that used by respiring heterotrophs, which transfer electrons from an organic molecule to oxygen. As electrons are passed along the electron transport chain to oxygen, a proton gradient is generated across the cell membrane. This gradient is used to generate molecules of ATP. Other reactions present in lithoautotrophs are those used for the removal of electrons from the inorganic donor and for carbon dioxide fixation.

PHOTOTROPHIC METABOLISM

Life on Earth is dependent on the conversion of solar energy to cellular energy by the process of photosynthesis. The general process of photosynthesis makes use of pigments called chlorophylls that absorb light energy from the Sun and release an electron with a higher energy level. This electron is passed through an electron transport chain, with the generation of energy by formation of a proton gradient and concomitant ATP synthesis. The electron ultimately returns to the chlorophyll. This cyclic reaction path can fulfill the energy needs of the cell. For the cell to grow, however, the Calvin cycle of carbon dioxide fixation must be activated, and electrons must be transferred to the cofactor NADP to form NADPH, which is needed in large amounts for

Warmer temperatures can cause cyanobacteria to spread across the surface of water, such as on this lake in China.

the operation of the cycle. Thus, phototrophic cell growth requires that a source of electrons be available to replace the electrons that are consumed during biosynthetic reactions.

Photosynthetic organisms are divided into two broad groups according to the nature of the source of these electrons. One group includes the higher plants, eukaryotic algae, and the cyanobacteria (blue-green algae); these organisms contain the pigment chlorophyll *a* and use water as their electron source in reactions that generate oxygen. It is thought that predecessors of the cyanobacteria carried out the global production of oxygen on the originally anoxic (absence of oxygen) Earth some 1.5 billion years ago, which made possible the development of higher forms of life. Oxygen-evolving photosynthesis requires the action of two separate light-absorbing systems to raise the energy of the electrons from water to a level high enough for their transfer to NADP. Thus, two distinct photoreaction centres are present in these organisms, one for the oxygen-generating reaction and the other for the cyclic process for energy generation. In the cyanobacteria, both photoreaction centres contain chlorophyll *a*. Their photosynthetic apparatus also contains other light-absorbing pigments that serve as antennae to capture light energy and transfer it to the reaction centres. Cyanobacterial antennae include additional molecules of chlorophyll *a*, which transfer energy to the cyclic reaction centre, and phycobilisomes, which are protein pigments that absorb light of short, high-energy wavelengths and transmit this energy to the oxygen-evolving reaction centre. In almost all cyanobacteria, the photosynthetic apparatus is contained in an extensive intracellular system of flattened membranous sacs, called thylakoids, the outer surfaces of which are studded with regular arrays of phycobilisome granules. This arrangement, in which pigment aggregates exist on the thylakoid surfaces, is called a photosystem.

Other photosynthetic bacteria contain only a single type of reaction centre with a different pigment, called bacteriochlorophyll, which absorbs light of long, low-energy wavelengths. These organisms require an electron donor other than water and do not release oxygen. The green bacteria (Chlorobiaceae) and purple sulfur bacteria (Chromatiaceae) use elemental sulfur, sulfide, thiosulfate, or hydrogen gas as electron donor, whereas the purple nonsulfur bacteria use electrons from hydrogen or organic substrates. These bacteria require anaerobic conditions for photosynthetic activity. The photosystem in

BIOSYNTHETIC PATHWAYS

Many prokaryotes are able to convert any given carbon source into biosynthetic building blocks—e.g., amino acids, purines, pyrimidines, lipids, sugars, and enzyme cofactors. The amount and activity of each enzyme in these biosynthetic pathways are carefully regulated so that the cell produces only as much of any compound as is needed at any time.

During the process of evolution, some bacteria have lost genes that encode certain biosynthetic reactions and are hence likely to require nutritional supplements. For example, *Mycoplasma*, whose DNA content is about one-quarter the size of that of *E. coli*, has many nutritional requirements and has even lost the ability to make a cell wall.

green bacteria is related to photosystem I of higher plants, whereas that in purple bacteria is related to photosystem II, which provides some indication of an evolutionary trail from bacteria to plants.

BIOFILMS

Biofilms are aggregates of bacteria held together by a mucus-like matrix of carbohydrate that adheres to a surface. Biofilms can form on the surfaces of liquids, solids, and living tissues, such as those of animals and plants. Communities form when individual organisms, which may be of the same or different species, adhere to and accumulate on a surface; this process is called adsorption. Following a period of growth and reproduction, the organisms produce an extracellular matrix consisting of carbohydrates called polysaccharides. This matrix serves to hold the bacteria together and to irreversibly bind them to the surface.

The communication of information concerning metabolism and population size by bacteria in biofilms relies on quorum sensing, which involves the production of small molecules called auto-inducers, or pheromones. The concentration of quorum-sensing molecules—most commonly peptides or acylated homoserine lactones (AHLs; special signaling chemicals)—is related to the number of bacteria of the same or different species that are in the biofilm and helps coordinate the behaviour of the biofilm. Biofilms are advantageous to bacteria because they provide a nutrient-rich environment that facilitates growth and because they confer resistance to antibiotics. Biofilms can cause severe infections in hospitalized patients; the formation of biofilms in these instances is typically associated with the introduction into the body of foreign substrates, such as artificial implants and urinary catheters. Biofilms also form on the thin films of plaque found on teeth, where they ferment sugars and starches into acids, causing the destruction of tooth enamel. In the environment, biofilms fill an important role in the breakdown of organic wastes by filtering wastes from water and by removing or neutralizing contaminants in soil. As a result, biofilms are used to purify water in water treatment plants and to detoxify contaminated areas of the environment.

DISTRIBUTION IN NATURE

Prokaryotes are ubiquitous on the Earth's surface. They are found in every accessible environment, from polar ice to bubbling hot springs, from mountaintops to the ocean floor, and from plant and animal bodies to forest soils. Some bacteria can grow in soil or water at temperatures near freezing (0 °C [32 °F]), whereas others thrive in water at temperatures near boiling (100 °C [212 °F]). Each bacterium is adapted to live in a particular environmental niche, be it oceanic surfaces, mud sediments, soil, or the surfaces of another organism. The level of bacteria in the air is low but significant, especially when dust has been suspended. In uncontaminated natural bodies of water, bacterial counts can be in the thousands per millilitre; in fertile soil, bacterial counts can be in the millions per gram; and in feces, bacterial counts can exceed billions per gram.

Prokaryotes are important members of their habitats. Although they are small in size, their sheer numbers mean that their metabolism plays an enormous role—sometimes beneficial, sometimes harmful—in the conversion of elements in their external environment. Probably every naturally occurring substance, and many synthetic ones, can be degraded (metabolized) by some species of bacteria (often members of the aerobic Pseudomonas groups). The largest stomach of the cow, the rumen, is a fermentation chamber in which bacteria digest the cellulose in grasses and feeds, converting them to fatty acids and amino acids, which are the fundamental nutrients used by the cow and the basis for the cow's production of milk. Organic wastes in sewage or compost piles are converted by bacteria either into suitable nutrients for plant metabolism or into gaseous methane (CH_4) and carbon dioxide. The remains of all organic materials, including plants and animals, are eventually converted to soil and gases through the activities of bacteria and other microorganisms and are thereby made available for further growth.

Many bacteria live in streams and other sources of water, and their presence at low population densities in a sample of water does not necessarily indicate that the water is unfit for consumption. However, water that contains bacteria such as *E. coli*, which are normal inhabitants of the intestinal tract of humans and animals, indicates that sewage or fecal material has recently polluted that water source. Such coliform bacteria may be pathogens themselves, and their presence signals that other, less easily detected bacterial and viral pathogens may also be present. Procedures used in water purification plants—settling, filtration, and chlorination—are designed to remove these and any other microorganisms and infectious agents that may be present in water that is intended for human consumption. Also, sewage treatment is necessary to prevent the release of pathogenic bacteria and viruses from wastewater into water supplies. Sewage treatment plants also initiate the decay of organic materials (proteins, fats, and carbohydrates) in the wastewater. The breakdown of organic material by microorganisms in the water consumes oxygen (biochemical oxygen demand), causing a decrease in the oxygen level, which can be very harmful to aquatic life in streams and lakes that receive the wastewater. One objective of sewage treatment is to oxidize as much organic material as possible before its discharge into the water system, thereby reducing the biochemical oxygen demand of the wastewater. Sewage digestion tanks and aeration devices specifically exploit the metabolic capacity of bacteria for this purpose.

Soil bacteria are extremely active in effecting biochemical changes by transforming the various substances, humus and minerals, that characterize soil. Elements that are central to life, such as carbon, nitrogen, and sulfur, are converted by bacteria from inorganic gaseous compounds into forms that can be used by plants and animals. Bacteria also convert the end products of plant and animal metabolism into forms that can be used by bacteria and other microorganisms. The nitrogen cycle can illustrate the role of bacteria in effecting various chemical changes. Nitrogen exists in nature in several oxidation states, as nitrate, nitrite, dinitrogen gas, several nitrogen oxides, ammonia, and organic amines (ammonia compounds containing one or more substituted hydrocarbons). Nitrogen fixation is the conversion of dinitrogen gas from the atmosphere into a form that can be used by living organisms. Some nitrogen-fixing bacteria, such as *Azotobacter*, *Clostridium pasteurianum*, and *Klebsiella pneumoniae*, are free-living, whereas species of *Rhizobium* live in an intimate association with leguminous plants. *Rhizobium* organisms in the soil recognize and invade the root hairs of their specific plant host, enter the plant tissues, and form a root nodule. This process causes the bacteria to lose many of their free-living characteristics. They become dependent upon the carbon supplied by the plant, and, in exchange for carbon, they convert nitrogen gas to ammonia, which is used by the plant for its protein synthesis and growth. In addition, many bacteria can convert nitrate to amines for purposes of synthesizing cellular materials or to ammonia when nitrate is used as electron acceptor. Denitrifying bacteria convert nitrate to dinitrogen gas. The conversion of ammonia or organic amines to nitrate is accomplished by the combined activities of the aerobic organisms *Nitrosomonas* and *Nitrobacter*, which use ammonia as an electron donor.

In the carbon cycle, carbon dioxide is converted into cellular materials by plants and autotrophic prokaryotes, and organic carbon is returned to the atmosphere by heterotrophic life-forms. The major breakdown product of microbial decomposition is carbon dioxide, which is formed by respiring aerobic organisms.

Methane, another gaseous end product of carbon metabolism, is a relatively minor component of the global carbon cycle but of importance in local situations and as a renewable energy source for human use. Methane production is carried out by the highly specialized and obligately anaerobic methanogenic prokaryotes, all of which are archaea. Methanogens use carbon dioxide as their terminal electron acceptor and receive electrons from hydrogen gas (H_2). A few other substances can be converted to methane by these organisms, including methanol, formic acid, acetic acid, and methylamines. Despite the extremely narrow range of substances that can be used by methanogens, methane production is very common during the anaerobic decomposition of many organic materials, including cellulose, starch, proteins, amino acids, fats, alcohols, and most other substrates. Methane formation from these materials requires that other anaerobic bacteria degrade these substances either to acetate or to carbon dioxide and hydrogen gas, which are then used by the methanogens. The methanogens support the growth of the other anaerobic bacteria in the mixture by removing hydrogen gas formed during their metabolic activities for methane production. Consumption of the hydrogen gas stimulates the metabolism of other bacteria.

Despite the fact that methanogens have such a restricted metabolic capability and are quite sensitive to oxygen, they are widespread on Earth. Large amounts of methane are produced in anaerobic environments, such as swamps and marshes, but significant amounts also are produced in soil and by ruminant animals. At least 80 percent of the methane in the atmosphere has been produced by the action of methanogens, the remainder being released from coal deposits or natural gas wells.

THE RELATIONSHIP BETWEEN BACTERIA AND HUMANS

The complexity of the relationship between humans and bacteria is reflected in the various ways in which humans simultaneously rely upon and defend against microorganisms. These interactions exist in various forms, including natural relationships (e.g., commensal bacteria that make up the normal flora of the human body) and industrial relationships (e.g., the production of certain foods and metals). Modern industrial applications stem largely from scientific investigations into the development of methods to harness the metabolic and biosynthetic properties of bacteria. In contrast, in the production of certain foods, humans have utilized bacteria for thousands of years, though the realization that bacteria played a role in these ancient processes has occurred only recently.

BACTERIA IN FOOD

Milk from a healthy cow initially contains very few bacteria, which primarily come from the skin of the cow and the procedures for handling the milk. Milk is an excellent growth medium for numerous bacteria, and the bacteria can increase rapidly in numbers unless the milk is properly processed. Bacterial growth can spoil the milk or even pose a serious health hazard if pathogenic bacteria are present. Diseases that can be transmitted from an infected cow include tuberculosis (*Mycobacterium tuberculosis*), undulant fever (*Brucella abortus*), and Q fever (*Coxiella burnetii*). In addition, typhoid fever (*Salmonella typhi*) can be transmitted through milk from an infected milk handler. Pasteurization procedures increase the temperature of the milk to 63 °C (145 °F) for 30 minutes or to

71 °C (160 °F) for 15 seconds, which kills any of the pathogenic bacteria that might be present, although these procedures do not kill all microorganisms.

Certain bacteria convert milk into useful dairy products, such as buttermilk, yogurt, and cheese. Commercially cultured buttermilk is prepared from skim milk inoculated with a starter culture of *Streptococcus lactis* or *S. cremoris*, together with *Leuconostoc citrovorum* or *L. dextranicum*. The combined action of *Streptococcus* and *Leuconos-*

This freeze-dried bacteria culture will be added to raw milk, along with rennet, to create cheese.

toc consumes the milk sugar, produces lactic acid, and precipitates milk protein (casein). Yogurt and other fermented milk products are produced in a similar manner using different cultures of bacteria. Many cheeses are likewise made through the action of bacteria. Growth in milk of an acid-producing bacterium such as *S. lactis* causes the casein to precipitate as curd. Following the removal of moisture and the addition of salt, the curd is allowed to ripen through the action of other microorganisms. Lactobacilli, streptococci, and propionibacteria are important for the ripening of Swiss cheese and the production of its characteristic taste and large gas bubbles. In addition, *Brevibacterium linens* is responsible for the flavour of Limburger cheese, and molds (*Penicillium* species) are used in the manufacture of Roquefort and Camembert cheeses. Other types of bacteria have long been used in the preparation and preservation of various foods produced through bacterial fermentation, including pickled products, sauerkraut, and olives.

The toxins of many pathogenic bacteria that are transmitted in foods can cause food poisoning when ingested. These include a toxin produced by *Staphylococcus aureus*, which causes a rapid, severe, but limited gastrointestinal distress, or the toxin of *Clostridium botulinum*, which is often

Substances Contributing to the Virulence of Pathogenic Bacteria	
substance	**action**
hyaluronidase	increases permeability of tissue spaces to bacterial
coagulase	increases resistance of bacteria to phagocytosis (engulfment by defense cells, or phagocytes)
hemolysins	destroys red blood cells
collagenase	dissolves collagen, a connective tissue protein
leucocidin	kills white blood cells (specifically leucocytes) and hence decreases phagocytic action
exotoxins and endotoxins	interferes with normal metabolic processes

lethal. Production of botulism toxin can occur in canned nonacidic foods that have been incompletely cooked before sealing. *C. botulinum* forms heat-resistant spores that can germinate into vegetative bacterial cells that thrive in the anaerobic environment, which is conducive to the production of their extremely potent toxin. Other food-borne infections are actually transmitted from an infected food handler, including typhoid fever, salmonellosis (*Salmonella* species), and shigellosis (*Shigella dysenteriae*).

BACTERIA IN INDUSTRY

Anaerobic sugar fermentation reactions by various bacteria produce different end products. The production of ethanol by yeasts has been exploited by the brewing industry for thousands of years and is used for fuel production. Specific bacteria carry out the oxidation of alcohol to acetic acid in the production of vinegar. Other fermentation processes make even more valuable products. Organic compounds, such as acetone, isopropanol, and butyric acid, are produced in fermentation by various *Clostridium* species and can been prepared on an industrial scale. Other bacterial products and reactions have been discovered in organisms from extreme environments. There is

Some Compounds Produced by Bacteria on an Industrial Scale

amylases	thermophilic *Bacillus* species	used in brewing to break down amyloses to maltoses
cellulases	*Clostridium thermocellus*	release of sugars from cellulose in waste from agriculture and papermaking
proteases (thermolysin, subtilisin, aqualysin)	*Thermus aquaticus* *Bacillus* species	used in brewing, baking, cheese processing, removal of hair from hides in the leather industry, and laundering
glucose isomerase	*Bacillus coagulans*	conversion of glucose to fructose as a sweetener in the food industry
beta-galactosidase	*Thermus aquaticus*	hydrolysis of lactose in milk whey to glucose and galactose
vinegar	*Acetobacter* species	from alcohol
monosodium glutamate	*Micrococcus* species	from sugar
dextran	*Leuconostoc mesenteroides*	from sucrose

considerable interest in the enzymes isolated from thermophilic bacteria, in which reactions may be carried out at higher rates owing to the higher temperatures at which they can occur.

Deposits of insoluble ferric iron (iron in the +3 oxidation state) are common in many environments. Bacterial reduction of ferric iron is common in waterlogged soils, bogs, and anaerobic portions of lakes. When the soluble ferrous iron (iron in the +2 oxidation state) thus formed reaches aerobic regions under neutral pH, the ferrous iron spontaneously oxidizes to insoluble, brown ferric deposits. In an acidic environment, iron does not readily oxidize from the ferrous to the ferric state. However, this reaction is tremendously accelerated by the acidophilic lithotrophic bacterium *Thiobacillus ferrooxidans*. When pyritic (ferrous sulfide) deposits are exposed to the air by mining operations, there is slow spontaneous oxidation of pyrite to ferrous ions and sulfuric acid. When the production of sulfuric acid causes conditions to reach a certain level of acidity, *T. ferrooxidans* thrives and oxidizes ferrous iron to the ferric form, which in turn oxidizes more pyrite in a continuously increasing fashion, with the formation of substantial amounts of sulfuric acid. The acidity of the environment may increase to a level near a pH of 2, which is a better environment for the solubilization of many other metal ions, particularly aluminum.

Some of the ferrous iron generated by the bacteria is carried away by groundwater into surrounding streams, making them acidic and loaded with iron, which precipitates and forms deposits of iron some distance downstream from the mine. Acid mine drainage would not develop in the absence of bacterial activity, and the only practical way to prevent its occurrence is to seal or cover the acid-bearing material to prevent exposure to air.

Although bacterial oxidation of sulfide materials results in the undesirable formation of acid mine drainage, the same reaction has been put to use for microbial leaching of copper, uranium, and other valuable metals from low-grade sulfide-containing ores. These metals are released from the ore after their conversion to more soluble forms by the direct oxidation of the metal by the bacterium and by the indirect oxidation of the metals in the ore by the ferric iron that was formed by bacterial action.

Microbial decomposition of petroleum products by hydrocarbon-oxidizing bacteria and fungi is of considerable ecological importance. The microbial decomposition of petroleum is an aerobic process, which is prevented if the oil settles to the layer of anaerobic sediment at the bottom (natural oil deposits in anaerobic environments are millions of years old). Hydrocarbon-oxidizing bacteria attach to floating oil droplets on the water surface, where their action eventually decomposes the oil to carbon dioxide. It is becoming a common practice to spray such bacteria and their growth factors onto oil spills to enhance the rate of degradation of the nonvolatile aliphatic and aromatic hydrocarbons.

BACTERIA IN MEDICINE

Bacterial diseases have played a dominant role in human history. Widespread epidemics of cholera and plague reduced populations of humans in some areas of the world by more than one-third. Bacterial pneumonia was probably the major cause of death in the aged. Perhaps more armies were defeated by typhus, dysentery, and other bacterial infections than by force of arms. With modern advances in plumbing and sanitation, the development of bacterial vaccines, and the discovery of antibacterial antibiotics, the incidence of bacterial disease has been reduced. Bacteria have not disappeared as infectious agents, however, since they continue to evolve, creating increasingly virulent strains and acquiring resistance to many antibiotics.

Although most bacteria are beneficial or even necessary for life on Earth, a few are known for their detrimental impact on humans. None of the Archaea are currently considered to be pathogens, but animals, including humans, are constantly bombarded and inhabited by large numbers and varieties of Bacteria. Most bacteria that contact an animal are rapidly eliminated by the host's defenses. The oral cavities, intestinal tract, and skin are colonized by enormous numbers of specific types of bacteria that are adapted to life in those habitats. These organisms are harmless under normal conditions and become dangerous only if they somehow pass across the barriers of the body and cause infection. Some bacteria are adept at invasion of a host and are called

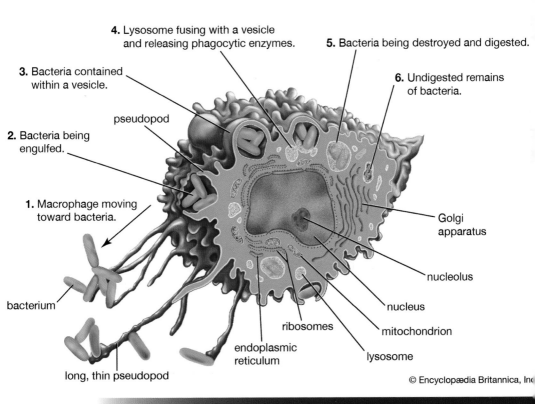

4. Lysosome fusing with a vesicle and releasing phagocytic enzymes.

5. Bacteria being destroyed and digested.

3. Bacteria contained within a vesicle.

6. Undigested remains of bacteria.

pseudopod

2. Bacteria being engulfed.

1. Macrophage moving toward bacteria.

Golgi apparatus

nucleolus

bacterium

nucleus

ribosomes

mitochondrion

endoplasmic reticulum

lysosome

long, thin pseudopod

© Encyclopædia Britannica, Inc

Macrophages, the principal phagocytic (cell-engulfing) components of the immune system, ingest and destroy foreign particles such as bacteria.

pathogens, or disease producers. Some pathogens act at specific parts of the body, such as meningo-coccal bacteria (*Neisseria meningitidis*), which invade and irritate the meninges, the membranes surround-ing the brain and spinal cord; the diphtheria bacterium (*Corynebacterium diphtheriae*), which initially infects the throat; and the cholera bacterium (*Vibrio chol-erae*), which reproduces in the intestinal tract, where the toxin that it produces causes the voluminous diarrhea characteristic of this cholera. Other bacte-ria that can infect humans include staphylococcal bacteria (primarily *Staphylococcus aureus*), which can infect the skin to cause boils (furuncles), the bloodstream to cause septicemia (blood poisoning), the heart valves to cause endocarditis, or the bones to cause osteomyelitis.

Pathogenic bacteria that invade an animal's bloodstream can use any of a number of mecha-nisms to evade the host's immune system, includ-ing the formation of long lipopolysaccharide chains to provide resistance to a group of serum immune proteins, called complement, that normally retard the bacterium. The pathogenic restructuring of bacterial surface proteins prevents antibodies produced by the animal from recognizing the pathogen and in some cases gives the patho-gen the ability to survive and grow in phagocytic white blood cells. Many pathogenic bacteria pro-duce toxins that assist them in invading the host.

Among these toxins are proteases, enzymes that break down tissue proteins, and lipases, enzymes that break down lipid (fat) and damage cells by disrupting their membranes. Other toxins disrupt cell membranes by forming a pore or channel in them. Some toxins are enzymes that modify specific proteins involved in protein synthesis or in control of host cell metabolism; examples include the diphtheria, cholera, and pertussis toxins.

Some pathogenic bacteria form areas in the host's body where they are closed off and protected from the immune system, as occurs in the boils in the skin formed by staphylococci and the cavities in the lungs formed by *Mycobacterium tuberculosis*. *Bacteroides fragilis* is the most numerous inhabitant of the human intestinal tract and causes no difficulties for the host as long as it remains there. If this bacterium gets into the body by means of an injury, the bacterial capsule stimulates the body to wall off the bacteria into an abscess, which reduces the spread of the bacteria. In many instances, the symptoms of bacterial infections are actually the result of an excessive response by the immune system rather than of the production of toxic factors by the bacterium.

Other means of combating pathogenic bacterial infections include the use of biotherapeutic agents, or probiotics. These are harmless bacteria that interfere with the colonization by pathogenic bacteria.

Another approach employs bacteriophages, viruses that kill bacteria, for the treatment of infections by specific bacterial pathogens. In addition, recombinant DNA technologies, developed during the 1980s, have made it possible to synthesize nearly any protein in bacteria, with *E. coli* serving as the usual host organism in this process. Recombinant DNA technology is used for the inexpensive, large-scale production of extremely scarce and valuable animal or human proteins, such as hormones, blood-clotting factors, and even antibodies.

EVOLUTION OF BACTERIA

Bacteria have existed from very early in the history of life on Earth. Bacteria fossils discovered in rocks date from at least the Devonian Period (416 to 359.2 million years ago), and there are convincing arguments that bacteria have been present since early Precambrian time, about 3.5 billion years ago. Bacteria were widespread on Earth at least since the middle of the Proterozoic Eon, about 1.5 billion years ago, when oxygen appeared in the atmosphere as a result of the action of the cyanobacteria. Bacteria have thus had plenty of time to adapt to their environments and to have given rise to numerous descendant forms.

The nature of the original predecessor involved in the origin of life is subject to considerable speculation. It has been suggested that the original cell might have used RNA as its genetic material, since investigations have shown that RNA molecules can have numerous catalytic functions. The Bacteria and Archaea diverged from their common precursor very early in this time period. The two types of prokaryotes tend to inhabit different types of environments and give rise to new species at different rates. Many Archaea prefer high-temperature niches. One major branch of the archaeal tree consists only of thermophilic species, and many of the methanogens in another major branch can grow at high temperatures. In contrast, no major eubacterial branch consists solely of thermophiles. Both Bacteria and Archaea contain members that are able to grow at very high temperatures, as well as other species that are able to grow at low temperatures. Another prominent difference is that bacteria have widely adapted to aerobic conditions, whereas many archaea are obligate anaerobes. No archaea are obligately photosynthetic. Perhaps the archaea are a more primitive type of organism with an impaired genetic response to changing environmental conditions. A limited ability to adapt to new situations could restrict the archaea to harsh environments, where there is less competition from other life-forms.

Organisms must evolve or adapt to changing environments, and it is clear that mutations, which are changes in the sequence of nucleotides in an organism's DNA, occur constantly in all organisms. The changes in DNA sequence might result in changes in the amino acid sequence of the protein that is encoded by that stretch of DNA. As a result, the altered protein might be either better-suited or less well-suited for function under the prevailing conditions. Although many nucleotide changes that can occur in DNA have no effect on the fitness of the cell, if the nucleotide change enhances the growth of that cell even by a small degree, then the mutant form would be able to increase its relative numbers in the population. If the nucleotide change retards the growth of the cell, however, then the mutant form would be outgrown by the other cells and lost.

The ability to transfer genetic information between organisms is a major factor in adaptation to changes in environment. The exchange of DNA is an essential part of the life cycle of higher eukaryotic organisms and can occur in all eukaryotes. Genetic exchange occurs throughout the bacterial world as well, and, although the amount of DNA that is transferred is small, this transfer can occur between distantly related organisms. Genes carried on plasmids can find their way onto the bacterial chromosome and become a stable part of the bacterium's inheritance. Organisms usually possess mobile genetic elements called transposons that can rearrange the order and presence of any genes on the chromosome. Transposons may play a role in helping to accelerate the pace of evolution.

Many examples of the rapid evolution of bacteria are available. Before the 1940s, antibiotics were not used in medical practice. When antibiotics did eventually come into use, the majority of pathogenic bacteria were sensitive to them. Since then, however, the bacterial resistance to one or more antibiotics has increased to the point that previously effective antibiotics are no longer useful against certain types of bacteria. Most examples of antibiotic resistance in pathogenic bacteria are not the result of a mutation that alters the protein that the antibiotic attacks, although this mechanism can occur. Instead, antibiotic resistance often involves the production by the bacterium of enzymes that alter the antibiotic and render it inactive. The major factor in the spread of antibiotic resistance is transmissible plasmids, which carry the genes for the drug-inactivating enzymes from one bacterial species to another. Although the original source of the gene for these enzymes is not known, mobile genetic elements (transposons) may have played a role in their appearance and may also allow their transfer to other bacterial types.

CHAPTER 3

TYPES OF BACTERIA

M illions of years of evolution have given rise to extraordinary metabolic diversity among prokaryotes, which is reflected in the countless different types of bacteria present on Earth. However, precisely how many different types of bacteria inhabit Earth is unknown. In fact, finding ways to accurately estimate the number of different bacterial species in various ecosystems, such as oceans and forest soils, is an important area of research. Understanding microbial diversity, which forms part of the larger endeavour of cataloguing all Earth's life-forms, promises to broaden scientists' knowledge of the fundamental roles of bacteria in nature and to identify new applications in biotechnology and industry.

METHODS OF CLASSIFICATION

Bacteria can be systematically separated into groups on the basis of morphological or shared evolutionary relationships. Today the classification of bacteria is grounded primarily in genetics. However, whereas genetic classification is valuable in understanding evolutionary relationships, morphological and bio-chemical features continue to play important roles in the functional identification and grouping of bacteria, particularly for the purposes of medicine.

CLASSIFICATION BY GENETICS

Genetic approaches to the classification of bacteria are aimed at identifying a degree of relatedness between organisms to obtain a more fundamental measure of the time elapsed since two organisms diverged from a common ancestor. The specific region of DNA that has proved to be the most infor-mative for evolutionary relatedness is *16S rRNA*, the gene that encodes the RNA component of the smaller subunit of the bacterial ribosome (16S refers to the rate of sedimentation, in Svedberg units, of the RNA molecule in a centrifugal field). The *16S rRNA* gene is present in all bacteria, and a related form occurs in all cells. The *16S rRNA* gene of *E. coli* is 1,542 nucleotides long, and some of its regions are double-stranded, while other regions are single-stranded. Single-stranded regions often form loops because there is a lack of complementary bases on the opposing strand. Since *16S rRNA* makes very specific contacts with many different ribosomal proteins and with other parts of itself, the pace at which spontaneous random mutation can change the sequence of the bases in the rRNA is slow. Any change in sequence at one site must be compensated for by another change elsewhere within the rRNA or in a ribosomal protein, lest the ribosome fail to assemble properly or to function in protein synthesis and the cell die.

Analysis of the *16S rRNA* sequences from many organisms has revealed that some portions of the molecule undergo rapid genetic changes, thereby distinguishing between different species within the same genus. Other positions change very slowly, allowing much broader taxonomic levels to be distinguished. The comparison of *16S rRNA* sequences between organisms is quantitative and is based on a defined set of assumptions. The assumption that the rate at which base changes occur and are established within a species is constant is unlikely to be true. Changes in the Earth's environment are expected to alter the ecological niches or selective pressures that affect the rate of mutation and the rate at which various species are able to evolve.

The radical differences between Archaea and Bacteria, which are evident in the composition of their lipids and cell walls and in the utilization of different metabolic pathways, enzymes, and enzyme cofactors, are also reflected in the rRNA sequences. The rRNAs of Bacteria and Archaea are as different from each other as they are from eukaryotic rRNA. This suggests that the bacterial and archaeal lines diverged from a common precursor somewhat before eukaryotic cells developed. This proposal also implies that the eukaryotic line is quite ancient and probably did not arise from any currently known bacteria. It had been previously believed that eukaryotic cells arose when some bacterial cells engulfed another type of bacterium. These bacteria might have formed a symbiotic relationship in which the engulfed cell continued to survive but gradually lost its independence and took on the properties of an organelle. Although the original eukaryotic cell may or may not be derived from bacteria, it remains likely, if not certain, that eukaryotic organelles (e.g., mitochondria and chloroplasts) are descendants of bacteria that were acquired by eukaryotic cells in an example of symbiotic parasitism. Early hypotheses about the origins of life suggested that the first cells obtained their energy from the breakdown of nutrients in a rich organic liquid environment proposed to have formed in the early oceans by the action of light and intense solar radiation on the early, anaerobic atmosphere. The process of photosynthesis might have evolved much later in response to the gradual depletion of those rich nutrient sources. On the other hand, rRNA sequence analysis places photosynthetic capability in almost all of the major bacterial divisions and shows that photosynthetic genera are closely related to nonphotosynthetic genera. Since photosynthesis is such a highly conserved, mechanistically complex process, it is unlikely that the ability to carry out photosynthesis could have evolved at different times in so many different organisms. Even more widely distributed among prokaryotes is lithotrophy (from the Greek word *lithos*, meaning "stone"), the ability to obtain energy by the transfer of electrons from hydrogen gas to inorganic acceptors. It has been proposed that the earliest forms of life on Earth used lithotrophic metabolism and that photosynthesis was a later addition to the early bacterial progenitors. The nonlithotrophic and nonphotosynthetic forms found today arose from the earliest forms of Bacteria, although they have lost their capacities for lithotrophy and photosynthesis.

The proposal that lithotrophy was widely distributed among bacterial organisms before photosynthesis developed suggests that the Archaea came from a different line of descent than Bacteria. The only photosynthetic archaeon, *Halobacterium*, has a completely different type of photosynthesis that does not use chlorophyll in large protein complexes to activate an electron, as in plants and bacteria. Rather, it uses a single protein, bacteriorhodopsin, in which light energy is absorbed by retinal, a form of vitamin A, to activate a proton (hydrogen ion).

The analysis of rRNA sequences from bacteria that are closely related to one another has revealed several surprising relationships between these organisms. For example, *Mycoplasma*, which appear to be different from other bacteria—in that they are very small, lack a cell wall, have a very small genome, and have sterols in their cell membranes— actually are related to some Gram-positive clostridia on the basis of their nucleic acid sequences. This circumstance underscores the hazard of relying on phenotypic traits (observable characteristics such as the absence of a cell wall) for the assignment of evolutionary or genetic relationships. In fact, there are many groupings of bacteria that are not supported by RNA sequence analysis.

CLASSIFICATION BY OTHER FEATURES

Although classification based on genetic divergence highlights the evolutionary relationships of bacteria, classification based on the morphological and biochemical features of bacteria remains the most practical way to identify these organisms. A definitive identification scheme for bacteria was first presented in 1984 in *Bergey's Manual of Systematic Bacteriology*. In this scheme, bacteria are classified on the basis of many characteristics. Cell shape, nature of multicell aggregates, motility, formation of spores, and reaction to the Gram stain are important. These morphological features, including the shape and colour of bacterial colonies, are not always constant and can be influenced by environmental conditions. Important in the identification of a genus and species of bacteria are biochemical tests, including the determination of the kinds of nutrients a cell can use, the products of its metabolism, the response to specific chemicals, and the presence of particular characteristic enzymes. Other criteria used for the identification of some types of bacteria might be their antigenic composition, habitat, disease production, and requirement for specific nutrients. Some tests are based on the ultrastructure of the bacteria revealed under the electron microscope by negative staining and preparation of thin sections.

MAJOR GROUPS OF GRAM-NEGATIVE BACTERIA

The nature of the bacterial cell wall serves as the major determinant for identifying the two primary morphological groups: Gram-negative bacteria and Gram-positive bacteria. These groups differ based on the thickness of the peptidoglycan layer in the cell wall and are easily distinguished under a microscope, since Gram-negative bacteria appear light pink, whereas Gram-positive bacteria appear purple. Gram-negative and Gram-positive bacteria are frequently described as being either spherically shaped or rod-shaped. This distinction is used to further categorize the organisms within their respective Gram groups. Though morphological groupings provide little information about the evolutionary history of bacteria, they provide very valuable information for the diagnosis and treatment of bacterial infections.

Gram-negative bacteria have only a thin peptidoglycan layer in their cells walls. As a result, since their cell walls are readily penetrated by solvent that removes purple dye utilized during Gram staining, they appear light pink in colour. There are a number of different kinds of Gram-negative bacteria, many of which are pathogenic in humans, including *E. coli*, *Salmonella*, and *Yersinia*.

CHLAMYDIA

Chlamydia is a genus of bacterial parasites that cause several different diseases in humans. The genus is composed of three species: *C. psittaci*, which causes psittacosis; *C. trachomatis*, various strains of which cause trachoma, lymphogranuloma venereum, and conjunctivitis; and *C. pneumoniae*, which causes respiratory-tract infections.

C. trachomatis also causes a variety of sexually transmitted diseases, chiefly nongonococcal urethritis (infection of the urethra) in males and females and epididymitis (infection of the epididymus) in males. In men, nongonococcal urethritis has symptoms similar to those of gonorrhea. A gonorrhea-like discharge from the penis is the most prominent symptom. Painful urination may occur but is usually less prominent than with gonorrhea. The symptoms of nongonococcal urethritis appear one to four weeks after the infection has been contracted through sexual intercourse.

A chlamydial infection ordinarily produces few if any symptoms in women. There may be a slight vaginal discharge and pelvic pain. If untreated, however, *C. trachomatis* can seriously infect the cervix (causing cervicitis), the urethra (causing urethritis), or the fallopian tubes (causing salpingitis), and it can also cause pelvic inflammatory disease. Infection of the fallopian tubes can cause sterility, and a chlamydial infection also leads to a higher risk of premature births, ectopic pregnancies, and postpartum infections. A woman with an infected cervix may give birth to infected newborns who can develop pneumonia or the eye disease known as neonatal conjunctivitis.

C. pneumoniae was identified as a separate *Chlamydia* species in the 1980s. It causes various respiratory-tract infections, most commonly a mild, atypical pneumonia with symptoms of fever, cough, and sore throat.

In diagnosis it is important to eliminate gonorrhea as a cause for the symptoms. Specific tests for *chlamydia* include smears and cultures. The preferred treatment for chlamydial infections is tetracycline. Erythromycin and sulfonamide drugs have also been effective in treating the infections. Appropriate treatment produces a speedy recovery.

CYANOBACTERIA

Cyanobacteria (also called blue-green algae) are any of a large, heterogeneous group of prokaryotic, principally photosynthetic organisms in the domain Bacteria. Cyanobacteria resemble the eukaryotic algae in many ways, including morphological characteristics and ecological niches, and were at one time treated as algae, hence the common name of blue-green algae. In fact, despite their placement in Bacteria, their taxonomic relationship to algae, plants, and protists remains unclear.

Like all other prokaryotes, cyanobacteria lack a membrane-bound nucleus, mitochondria, Golgi apparatus, chloroplasts, and endoplasmic reticulum. All of the functions carried out in eukaryotes by these membrane-bound organelles are carried out in prokaryotes by the bacterial cell membrane. Some cyanobacteria, especially planktonic forms, have gas vesicles that contribute to their buoyancy. Chemical, genetic, and physiological characteristics are used to further classify the group within the kingdom. Cyanobacteria may be unicellular or filamentous. Many have sheaths to bind other cells or filaments into colonies.

Cyanobacteria contain only one form of chlorophyll, chlorophyll *a*, a green pigment. In addition, they contain various yellowish carotenoids, the blue pigment phycobilin, and, in some species, the red pigment phycoerythrin. The combination of phycobilin and chlorophyll produces the characteristic blue-green colour from which these organisms derive their popular name. Because of the other pigments, however, many species are actually green, brown, yellow, black, or red.

Most cyanobacteria do not grow in the absence of light (i.e., they are obligate phototrophs). However, some can grow in the dark if there is a sufficient supply of glucose to act as a carbon and energy source. In addition to being photosynthetic, many species of cyanobacteria can also "fix" atmospheric nitrogen— that is, they can transform the gaseous nitrogen of the air into compounds that can be used by living cells. Particularly efficient nitrogen fixers are found among the filamentous species that have specialized cells called heterocysts. The heterocysts are thick-walled cell inclusions that are impermeable to oxygen; they provide the anaerobic (oxygen-free) environment necessary for the operation of the nitrogen-fixing enzymes. In Southeast Asia, nitrogen-fixing cyanobacteria often are grown in rice paddies, thereby eliminating the need to apply nitrogen fertilizers.

Cyanobacteria range in size from 0.5 to 60 μm (micrometre; 1 μm = 10^{-6} metre = 0.000039 inch), which represents the largest prokaryotic organism. They are widely distributed and are extremely common in fresh water, where they occur as members of both the plankton and the benthos. They are also abundantly represented in habitats such as tide pools, coral reefs, and tidal spray zones. A few species also occur in the ocean plankton. On land, cyanobacteria are common in soil down to a depth of 1 metre (3.3 feet) or more. They also grow on moist surfaces of rocks and trees, where they appear in the form of cushions or layers.

Cyanobacteria flourish in some of the most inhospitable environments known. They can be found in hot springs, in cold lakes underneath 5 metres (16.4 feet) of ice pack, and on the lower surfaces of many rocks in deserts. Cyanobacteria are frequently among the first colonizers of bare rock and soil. Various types of associations take place between cyanobacteria and other organisms. Certain species, for example, grow in a mutualistic relationship with fungi, forming composite organisms known as lichens.

Cyanobacteria reproduce asexually, either by means of binary or multiple fission in unicellular and colonial forms or by fragmentation and spore formation in filamentous species. Under favourable conditions, cyanobacteria can reproduce at explosive rates, forming dense concentrations called blooms. Cyanobacteria blooms can colour a body of water. For example, many ponds take on an opaque shade of green as a result of overgrowths of cyanobacteria, and blooms of phycoerythrin-rich species cause the occasional red colour of the Red Sea. Cyanobacteria blooms are especially common in waters that have been polluted by nitrogen wastes; in such cases, the overgrowths of cyanobacteria can consume so much of the water's dissolved oxygen that fish and other aquatic organisms perish.

Spirulina, a genus of cyanobacteria, is used as a traditional food source in parts of Africa and Mexico. It is an exceptionally rich source of vitamins, minerals, and protein, and one of the few nonanimal sources of vitamin B12. It has been widely studied for its possible antiviral, anti-cancer, antibacterial, and antiparasitic properties, and has been used for such medical conditions as allergies, ulcers, anemia, heavy-metal poisoning, and radiation poisoning. It is also used in weight-loss programs.

ENTEROBACTER

Enterobacter is a genus of rod-shaped bacteria of the family Enterobacteriaceae. *Enterobacter* are Gram-negative bacteria that are classified as facultative anaerobes, meaning they are able to thrive in both aerobic and anaerobic environments. Many species possess flagella and thus are motile. Features such as motility, as well as certain biochemical properties (including the ability to synthesize an enzyme known as ornithine decarboxylase), are used to distinguish *Enterobacter* from the very similar and closely related *Klebsiella* bacteria. *Enterobacter* is named for the organisms' predominant natural habitat, the intestines of animals (from Greek *enteron*, meaning "intestine").

Enterobacter are ubiquitous in nature; their presence in the intestinal tracts of animals results in their wide distribution in soil, water, and sewage. They are also found in plants. In humans, multiple *Enterobacter* species are known to act as opportunistic pathogens, including: *E. cloacae, E. aerogenes, E. sakazakii, E. gergoviae,* and *E. agglomerans.* Pathogenic *Enterobacter* can cause any of a variety of conditions, including eye and skin infections, meningitis, bacteremia (bacterial blood infection), pneumonia, and urinary tract infections. In many instances, illness caused by *E. cloacae* or by *E. aerogenes* is associated with exposure to the organisms in nosocomial settings, such as hospitals or nursing homes.

The emergence of drug-resistant *Enterobacter* organisms has complicated treatment regimens, particularly within nosocomial settings, where such organisms have become increasingly common. Traditional approaches to treating *Enterobacter* infections involve single-agent antimicrobial therapy, typically with an aminoglycoside, a fluoroquinolone, a cephalosporin, or imipenem. In some instances, however, subpopulations of *Enterobacter* are capable of producing enzymes known as beta-lactamases, which cleave the central ring structure responsible for the activity of beta-lactam antibiotics, a group that includes imipenem and cephalosporins. Exposure to these drugs kills off organisms that do not produce the enzyme but leaves behind beta-lactamase-synthesizing *Enterobacter*, thereby selecting for drug-resistant populations of organisms. Newer approaches to *Enterobacter* infections have adopted combination-therapy regimens employing multiple antibiotics with different core structures, such as an aminoglycoside or a fluoroquinolone in combination with a beta-lactam agent. Despite the promise of this more diverse strategy, however, it has been associated with the selection of multi-drug resistant organisms.

Resistance of *Enterobacter* to non-beta-lactam antibiotics, including fluoroquinolones such as ciprofloxacin, involves distinct cellular and genetic mechanisms. Examples of bacteria utilizing such mechanisms include ciprofloxacin-resistant *E.*

aerogenes and multidrug-resistant *E. aerogenes*, which in many instances is resistant to ciprofloxacin and imipenem. In *Enterobacter* organisms resistant to aminoglycosides, resistance has been associated with a bacterial genetic element known as an integron. Integrons contain genes that confer antibiotic resistance capabilities and are incorporated into bacterial genomes via genetic recombination. They are efficiently exchanged and disseminated among circulating bacterial populations, such as those occurring in nosocomial environments. In *E. cloacae* resistance to the aminoglycoside gentamicin has been attributed to the presence of integrons in the organism's genome.

Free-living *Enterobacter* are capable of nitrogen fixation. Certain species, notably *E. cloacae*, are involved in symbiotic nitrogen fixation in plants and have been isolated from the root nodules of certain crops, such as wheat and sorghum, and from the rhizospheres of rice.

ESCHERICHIA

Escherichia coli is a species of bacterium that normally inhabits the stomach and intestines. When *E. coli* is consumed in contaminated water, milk, or food or is transmitted through the bite of a fly or other insect, it can cause gastrointestinal illness.

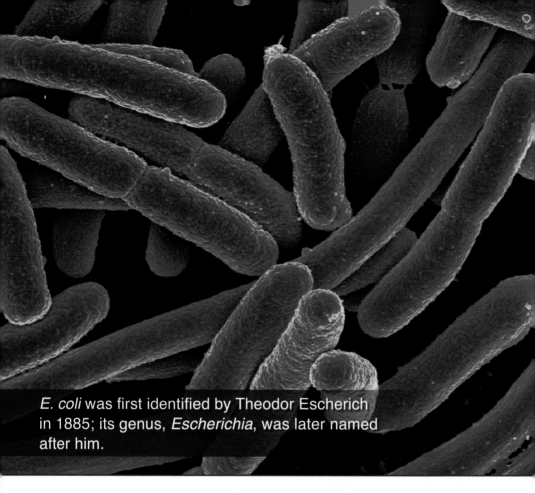

E. coli was first identified by Theodor Escherich in 1885; its genus, *Escherichia*, was later named after him.

Mutations can lead to strains that cause diarrhea by giving off toxins, invading the intestinal lining, or sticking to the intestinal wall. Therapy for gastrointestinal illness consists largely of fluid replacement, though specific drugs are effective in some cases. The illness is usually self-limiting, with no evidence of long-lasting effects. However, one dangerous strain causes bloody diarrhea, kidney failure, and death in extreme cases. Proper cooking of meat and washing of produce can prevent infection from contaminated food sources. *E. coli* also can cause urinary tract infections in women.

KLEBSIELLA

Klebsiella is a genus of rod-shaped bacteria of the family Enterobacteriaceae. *Klebsiella* organisms are categorized microbiologically as Gram-negative, facultative anaerobic, nonmotile bacteria. *Klebsiella* organisms occur in soil and water and on plants, and some strains are considered a part of the normal flora of the human gastrointestinal tract. The genus is named for German physician and bacteriologist Edwin Klebs.

Klebsiella pneumoniae, also called Friedländer's *bacillus*, was first described in 1882 by German microbiologist and pathologist Carl Friedländer. *K. pneumoniae* is best known as a pathogen of the human respiratory system that causes pneumonia. The disease is usually seen only in patients with underlying medical problems such as alcoholism or chronic pulmonary disease and often arises as a nosocomial infection (infection occurring in association with invasive treatment or long-term care in hospitals or other community health-care settings).

Traditionally, the bacteria *K. ozaenae* and *K. rhinoscleromatis* were recognized as separate species, but DNA studies indicate that they should be classified as subspecies of *K. pneumoniae*; for medical purposes, the species distinctions are still observed, however. Other *Klebsiella* species include *K. oxytoca* and *K. planticola*, which along with *K. pneumoniae* can cause human urinary tract and wound infections. *K. planticola* and certain strains of *K. pneumoniae* have been isolated from the roots of plants such as wheat, rice, and corn (maize), where they act as nitrogen-fixing bacteria.

K. variicola, which was discovered in 2004, also occurs on various plants, including rice, banana, and sugar cane. This species of bacteria has also been isolated from hospital settings, where it may act as an opportunistic pathogen, similar to other *Klebsiella* organisms.

Although some *Klebsiella* infections can be effectively treated with single-agent therapy involving penicillin or a similar antibiotic, the emergence of organisms that are resistant to these drugs has necessitated the development of novel therapeutic approaches. For example, *K. pneumoniae* is resistant to beta-lactam antibiotics, a group that includes carbapenems, penicillins, and cephalosporins. Resistance results from the organism's ability to synthesize an enzyme known as carbapenemase, which hydrolyzes the beta-lactam ring that underlies the antimicrobial activity of these drugs. As a result, drug-resistant *K. pneumoniae* infections typically require combination therapy with structurally diverse agents, such as a beta lactam antibiotic and an aminoglycoside.

NITROGEN-FIXING BACTERIA

Nitrogen-fixing bacteria are capable of transforming atmospheric nitrogen into fixed nitrogen, an inorganic compound that can be utilized by plants. More than 90 percent of all nitrogen fixation is effected by these microorganisms.

Two kinds of nitrogen fixers are recognized. The first kind consists of free-living (non-symbiotic) bacteria, including the cyanobacteria *Anabaena* and Nostoc and genera such as *Azotobacter*, *Beijerinckia*, and *Clostridium*. The second kind consists of mutualistic (symbiotic) bacteria, such as *Rhizobium*, associated with leguminous plants, and *Spirillum lipoferum*, associated with cereal grasses.

The symbiotic nitrogen-fixing bacteria invade the root hairs of host plants, where they multiply and stimulate formation of root nodules, enlargements of plant cells and bacteria in intimate association. Within the nodules the bacteria convert free nitrogen to nitrates, which the host plant utilizes for its development. To insure sufficient nodule formation and optimum growth of legumes (e.g., alfalfa, beans, clovers, peas, soybeans), seeds are usually inoculated with commercial cultures of appropriate *Rhizobium* species, especially in soils poor or lacking in the required bacterium.

PASTEURELLA

Pasteurella is a genus of rod-shaped bacteria that causes several serious diseases in domestic animals and milder infections in humans. The genus was named after Louis Pasteur. Its species are microbiologically characterized as Gram-negative, nonmotile, facultative anaerobes (not requiring oxygen) that have a fermentative type of metabolism. They are 0.3–1 μm across by 1–2 μm long.

Louis Pasteur, one of the most important founders of medical microbiology, originated the process of pasteurization, by which liquids such as milk are heated to destroy bacteria that cause disease or spoilage.

The infections they cause, referred to by the general term *pasteurelloses*, are widespread, being transmitted by direct contact and, in some cases, by certain species of ticks and fleas. The genus is closely related to the genera *Haemophilus* and *Actinobacillus*, and together the three genera form the family Pasteurellaceae.

Pasteurella multocida is pathogenic for many animals, causing fowl cholera, blood poisoning in ruminants, pneumonia in young cattle, and respiratory infection in cattle and humans. It is also the cause of shipping fever, which commonly attacks animals under stress, as during shipping. In this disease, fever is followed by respiratory difficulty, which may lead to pneumonia and more severe symptoms. Treatment includes isolation, rest, and antibiotic therapy. *P. haemolytica* is a cause of sheep pneumonia.

P. multocida and *P. dagmatis* are also often found in the mouths of healthy cats and dogs and can cause infection in bite wounds of those animals.

The agents of tularemia and bubonic plague, previously designated *P. tularensis* and *P. pestis*, respectively, have been reclassified as *Francisella tularensis* and *Yersinia pestis*. Control by vaccine is variable, as is treatment with penicillin and other antibiotics, such as tetracycline.

PSEUDOMONADS

Pseudomonads are bacteria of the family Pseudo-monadaceae, a large and varied group comprising four major genera and several hundred species. The individual cells are rod-shaped, often curved, averaging about 1 μm in diameter and several micrometres in length. The cells of most species are separate and not joined in filaments; many are motile, propelled by one or more flagella, usually located terminally. The cells of some aquatic species are attached to surfaces by long strands or stalks (holdfasts).

Most species of the family are found in soil or water; some cause diseases in plants, and a few cause serious diseases in humans and other mammals. *Pseudomonas aeruginosa*, very common and widespread, is an opportunistic pathogen in humans and may be resistant to certain antibiotics. It has been implicated in hospital-acquired infections of surgical wounds and severely burned tissue and in fatal infections of cancer patients treated with immunosuppressive drugs. *Burkholderia mallei*, the cause of glanders, or farcy, of horses and donkeys, is occasionally pathogenic in humans, and *B. pseudomallei* causes melioidosis, an uncommon but highly fatal tropical lung disease of humans and other mammals. *B. cepacia*, similar to *P. aeruginosa*, is a cause of serious lung infections in people with cystic fibrosis.

Some pseudomonads cause plant diseases. For example, *P. syringae* causes disease in lilacs, citrus, beans, and cherries, and *Ralstonia solanacearum* causes disease in potato, tomato, tobacco, and other plants. *Xanthomonas* is distinct among bacteria for its unique yellowish cell pigments. Its species cause bacterial spot of peach (*X. pruni*) and tomato (*X. vescicatoria*), canker of grapevine (*X. ampelina*), and a number of vascular diseases of cole crops (*X. campestris*).

RICKETTSIA

Rickettsiae belong to one of three genera, *Rickettsia*, *Coxiella*, or *Rochalimaea*, in the bacteria family Rickettsiaceae. The rickettsiae are rod-shaped or variably spherical, nonfilterable bacteria, and most species are Gram-negative. They are natural parasites of certain arthropods (notably lice, fleas, mites, and ticks) and can cause serious diseases—usually characterized by acute, self-limiting fevers—in humans and other animals.

The rickettsiae range in size from roughly 0.3–0.5 μm by 0.8–2.0 μm. Virtually all rickettsiae can reproduce only within animal cells. Rickettsiae are usually transmitted to humans by a bite from an arthropod carrier. Because certain species can withstand considerable drying, transmission of rickettsia can also occur when arthropod feces are inhaled or enter the skin through abrasion. Most rickettsiae normally infect animals other than humans, who become involved as dead-end hosts only accidentally. Epidemic typhus and trench fever are exceptions, since humans are the only host of proven importance. The other rickettsial infections occur primarily in animals, which serve as reservoirs from which bloodsucking arthropods acquire the rickettsial bacteria and in turn transmit them to other animals and, occasionally, humans.

The largest rickettsial genus, *Rickettsia*, is generally subdivided into the typhus group, the spotted fever group, and the scrub typhus group. This genus alone is responsible for a number of highly virulent diseases including Rocky Mountain spotted fever, epidemic typhus, Brill-Zinsser disease, scrub typhus, and others.

Protective measures against rickettsial disease agents include the control of arthropod carriers when necessary and immunization. Animals that recover from a rickettsiosis exhibit long-lasting immunity. Artificial immunity, as a preventive, is variably effective, typhus and the spotted fevers being among the easiest to immunize against. The most effective treatment of most rickettsioses includes the timely and prolonged administration of large amounts of broad-spectrum antibiotics such as tetracycline or, if tetracycline cannot be used, chloramphenicol.

SALMONELLA

Salmonella is a genus of rod-shaped, Gram-negative, facultatively anaerobic bacteria in the family Enterobacteriaceae.

Their principal habitat is the intestinal tract of humans and other animals. Some species exist in animals without causing disease symptoms; others can result in any of a wide range of mild to serious infections termed *salmonellosis* in humans. Most

This microbiologist is testing lettuce for *Salmonella* and *E. coli* after an outbreak of food-related illness.

human infections with *Salmonella* result from the ingestion of contaminated food or water. *Salmonella typhi* causes typhoid fever. Paratyphoid fever is caused by *S. paratyphi*, *S. schottmuelleri*, and *S. hirschfeldii*, which are considered variants of *S. enteritidis*. Refrigeration prevents bacterial reproduction but does not kill these microorganisms. As a result, many *Salmonella* can develop in foods, which, when ingested, can result in gastroenteritis.

SPIROCHETE

Spirochetes are any of a group of spiral-shaped bacteria, some of which are serious pathogens for humans, causing such diseases as syphilis, yaws, Lyme disease, and relapsing fever. Spirochetes include the genera *Spirochaeta*, *Treponema*, *Borrelia*, and *Leptospira*. Spirochetes are Gram-negative, motile, spiral bacteria, from 3 to 500 μm long. Spirochetes are unique in that they have endocellular flagella (axial fibrils, or axial filaments), which number between 2 and more than 200 per organism, depending upon the species. Each axial fibril attaches at an opposite end and winds around the cell body, which is enclosed by an envelope. Spirochetes are characteristically found in a liquid environment (e.g., mud and water, blood and lymph).

Treponema includes the agents of syphilis (*T. pallidum*) and yaws (*T. pertenue*). *Borrelia* includes

LYME DISEASE

Lyme disease is a tick-borne bacterial disease that was first conclusively identified in 1975 and is named for the town in Connecticut in which it was first observed. The disease has been identified in every region of the United States and in Europe, Asia, Africa, and Australia.

Lyme disease is caused by several closely related spirochetes, including *Borrelia burgdorferi* in the United States, *B. mayonii* in the upper Midwestern United States, and *B. afzelii* and *B. garinii* in Europe and Asia. The spirochetes are transmitted to the human bloodstream by the bite of various species of ticks. In the northeastern United States, the carrier tick is usually *Ixodes scapularis* (*I. dammini*); in the West, *I. pacificus*; and in Europe, *I. ricinus*. Ticks pick up the spirochete by sucking the blood of deer or other infected animals. *I. scapularis* mainly feeds on white-tailed deer and white-footed mice, especially in areas of tall grass, and is most active in summer. The larval and nymphal stages of this tick are more likely to bite humans than are the adult and are therefore more likely to cause human cases of the disease.

In humans, Lyme disease progresses in three stages, though symptoms and severity of illness vary depending on which type of *Borrelia* is involved. In *B. burgdorferi* infections, the first and mildest stage is characterized by a circular rash in

(continued on the next page)

(continued from the previous page)

a bull's-eye pattern that appears anywhere from a few days to a month after the tick bite. The rash is often accompanied by flulike symptoms, such as headache, fatigue, chills, loss of appetite, fever, and aching joints or muscles. The majority of persons who contract Lyme disease experience only these first-stage symptoms and never become seriously ill. A minority, however, will go on to the second stage of the disease, which begins two weeks to three months after infection. This stage is indicated by arthritic pain that migrates from joint to joint and by disturbances of memory, vision, movement, or other neurological symptoms. The third stage of Lyme disease, which generally begins within two years of the bite, is marked by crippling arthritis and by neurological symptoms that resemble those of multiple sclerosis. Symptoms vary widely, however, and some persons experience facial paralysis, meningitis, memory loss, mood swings, and an inability to concentrate.

Because Lyme disease often mimics other disorders, its diagnosis is sometimes difficult, especially when there is no record of the distinctive rash. Early treatment of Lyme disease with antibiotics is important in order to prevent progression of the disease to a more serious stage. More powerful antibiotics are used in the latter case, though symptoms may recur periodically thereafter.

several species transmitted by lice and ticks and causing relapsing fever (*B. recurrentis* and others) and Lyme disease (*B. burgdorferi*) in humans. *Spirochaeta* are free-living, nonpathogenic inhabitants of mud and water, usually in oxygen-free regions. Leptospirosis, caused by *Leptospira*, is principally a disease of domestic and wild mammals and is a secondary infection of humans.

SULFUR BACTERIA

Sulfur bacteria are any of a diverse group of microorganisms capable of metabolizing sulfur and its compounds and important in the sulfur cycle in nature. Some of the common sulfur substances that are used by these bacteria as an energy source are hydrogen sulfide (H_2S), sulfur, and thiosulfate ($S_2O_2^-$). The final product of sulfur oxidation is sulfate (SO_2^-).

Thiobacillus, widespread in marine and terrestrial habitats, oxidizes sulfur, producing sulfates useful to plants; in deep ground deposits it generates sulfuric acid, which dissolves metals in mines but also corrodes concrete and steel. *Desulfovibrio desulficans* reduces sulfates in waterlogged soils and sewage to hydrogen sulfide, a gas with the rotten egg odour so common to such places. *Thiothrix*, common in sulfur springs and in sewage, and *Sulfolobus*, confined to sulfur-rich hot springs, transform hydrogen sulfide to elemental sulfur. Many species in the families Chromatiaceae (purple sulfur bacteria) and Chlorobiaceae (green sulfur bacteria) utilize energy from light in an oxygen-free environment to transform sulfur and its compounds to sulfates.

VIBRIO

Vibrio is a genus of comma-shaped bacteria in the family Vibrionaceae. *Vibrio* are aquatic microorganisms, some species of which cause serious diseases in humans and other animals. They are microbiologically characterized as Gram-negative, highly motile, facultative anaerobes (not requiring oxygen), with one to three whiplike flagella at one end. Their cells are curved rods 0.5 μm across and 1.5 to 3.0 μm long, single or strung together in S-shapes or spirals.

Three species of Vibrio are of significance to humans: *V. cholerae* is the cause of cholera, and *V. parahaemolyticus* and *V. vulnificus* both act as agents of acute enteritis, or bacterial diarrhea. *V. anguillarum* is found in diseased eels and other fishes.

YERSINIA

Yersinia is a genus of ovoid- or rod-shaped bacteria of the family Enterobacteriaceae. *Yersinia* are Gram-negative bacteria and are described as facultative anaerobes, meaning they are capable of surviving in both aerobic and anaerobic environments. Though several species are motile below 37 °C (98.6 °F), all *Yersinia* organisms are rendered nonmotile at this temperature and above. The genus is named for French bacteriologist Alexandre Yersin, who in 1894 discovered *Pasteurella pestis* (now *Yersinia pestis*), the causative agent of plague, which was independently isolated that same year by Japanese physician and bacteriologist Kitasato Shibasaburo.

In addition to *Y. pestis*, other species that are important pathogens in humans include *Y. enterocolitica* and *Y. pseudotuberculosis*. *Y. enterocolitica* is widespread in domestic animals, including pigs and cattle, and is found in birds and in aquatic species, such as frogs and oysters. It also has been isolated from soil and from the surface layers of various bodies of water, including lakes and streams; its entry into soil and water systems originates with animal wastes. The organism is transmitted to humans as a foodborne or waterborne pathogen, and infection results in an acute gastrointestinal condition known as yersiniosis. A similar condition arises following infection with *Y. pseudotuberculosis*; however, little is known about its mode of transmission to humans. *Y. pseudotuberculosis* appears to circulate in a variety of animals and has been found in horses, cattle, dogs, cats, rabbits, rodents, deer, and birds, including ducks, geese, turkeys, and canaries. In some instances, infection with either *Y. pseudotuberculosis* or *Y. enterocolitica* may give rise to mesenteric lymphadenitis, an inflammation of the peritoneal tissue of the intestines that produces symptoms similar to those of appendicitis. In contrast to the other *Yersinia* organisms, *Y. pestis* circulates in rodents and is transmitted to humans through the bite of an infected flea.

Several other *Yersinia* organisms have been identified, including *Y. intermedia*, *Y. frederiksenii*, and *Y. ruckeri*. The latter is pathogenic in salmonids (family Salmonidae), including rainbow trout and Pacific salmon. In these species, *Y. ruckeri* causes enteric redmouth disease, which is characterized by hemorrhaging of the subcutaneous tissues under the fins and around the eyes and mouth.

MAJOR GROUPS OF GRAM-POSITIVE BACTERIA

Gram-positive bacteria are distinguished from Gram-negative organisms by the thick peptidoglycan layer in their cell walls. Dye that enters the cells during Gram staining is retained after treatment with a solvent, which is unable to penetrate through the cell wall to remove the stain. As a result, Gram-positive bacteria are purple in colour when viewed under the microscope following staining. Examples of important groups of Gram-positive organisms include *Lactobacillus, Staphylococcus,* and *Streptococcus.*

ACTINOMYCETES

Actinomycetes are Gram-positive, generally anaerobic bacteria noted for a filamentous and branching growth pattern that results, in most forms, in an extensive colony, or mycelium. The mycelium in some species may break apart to form rod- or coccoid-shaped forms. Many genera also form spores. The sporangia, or spore cases, may be found on aerial hyphae, on the colony surface, or free within the environment. Motility, when present, is conferred by flagella. Many species of actinomycetes occur in soil and are harmless to animals and higher plants, while some are important pathogens, and many others are beneficial sources of antibiotics.

Many authorities recognize eight different groups of actinomycetes, though these groups are themselves heterogeneous and will require further study to classify fully. Of the specific types of actinomycetes, *Nocardia asteroides* causes tissue infections in humans, and *Dermatophilus congolensis* causes dermatophilosis, a severe dermatitis of cattle, sheep, horses, and occasionally humans. Several species of *Streptomyces* cause the disease actinomycosis in humans and cattle. Many of the actinomycetes are sources of antibiotics such as streptomycin.

BACILLUS

Bacillus is a genus of rod-shaped, Gram-positive, aerobic or (under some conditions) anaerobic bacteria widely found in soil and water. The term *bacillus* has been applied in a general sense to all cylindrical or rodlike bacteria. The largest species are about 2 µm across by 7 µm long and frequently occur in chains.

In 1877 German botanist Ferdinand Cohn described two different forms of hay bacillus (now known as *Bacillus subtilis*): one that could be killed upon exposure to heat and one that was resistant to heat. He called the heat-resistant forms "spores" (endospores) and discovered that these dormant forms could be converted to a vegetative, or actively growing, state. Today it is known that all *Bacillus* species can form dormant spores under adverse environmental conditions. These endospores may remain viable for long periods of time. Endospores are resistant to heat, chemicals, and sunlight and are widely distributed in nature, primarily in soil, from which they invade dust particles.

Some types of *Bacillus* bacteria are harmful to humans, plants, or other organisms. For example, *B. cereus* sometimes causes spoilage in canned foods and food poisoning of short duration. *B. subtilis* is a common contaminant of laboratory cultures (it plagued Louis Pasteur in many of his experiments) and is often found on human skin. Most strains of

Bacillus are not pathogenic for humans but may, as soil organisms, infect humans incidentally. A notable exception is *B. anthracis*, which causes anthrax in humans and domestic animals. *B. thuringiensis* produces a toxin (Bt toxin) that causes disease in insects.

Medically useful antibiotics are produced by *B. subtilis* (bacitracin) and *B. polymyxa* (polymyxin B). In addition, strains of *B. amyloliquefaciens* bacteria, which occur in association with certain plants, are known to synthesize several different antibiotic substances, including bacillaene, macrolactin, and difficidin. These substances serve to protect the host plant from infection by fungi or other bacteria and are being studied for their usefulness as biological pest-control agents.

A gene encoding an enzyme known as barnase in *B. amyloliquefaciens* is of interest in the development of genetically modified (GM) plants. Barnase acts to kill plant cells that have become infected by fungal pathogens; this activity limits the spread of disease. The gene controlling production of the Bt toxin in *B. thuringiensis* has been used in the development of GM crops such as Bt cotton.

LACTOBACILLUS

Lactobacillus is a genus of rod-shaped, Gram-positive, non-spore-forming bacteria of the family Lactobacillaceae. Similar to other genera in the family, *Lactobacillus* are characterized by their ability to produce lactic acid as a by-product of glucose metabolism. The organisms are widely distributed in animal feeds, silage, manure, and milk and milk products. Various species of *Lactobacillus* are used commercially during the production of sour milks, cheeses, and yogurt, and they have an important role in the manufacture of fermented vegetables (pickles and sauerkraut), beverages (wine and juices), sourdough breads, and some sausages.

Lactobacillus are generally nonmotile and can survive in both aerobic and anaerobic environments. *L. delbrueckii*, the type species of the genus, is 0.5 to 0.8 μm across by 2 to 9 μm long and occurs singly or in small chains. Examples of other well-characterized *Lactobacillus* species include *L. acidophilus*, *L. brevis*, *L. casei*, and *L. sanfranciscensis*.

The amount of lactic acid produced by different *Lactobacillus* organisms varies. In several species, including *L. acidophilus*, *L. casei*, and *L. plantarum*, glucose metabolism is described as homofermentative, since lactic acid is the primary byproduct, representing at least 85 percent of end metabolic products. However, in other species, such as *L. brevis* and *L. fermentum*, glucose metabolism is heterofermentative, with lactic acid making up about 50 percent of metabolic byproducts and ethanol, acetic acid, and carbon dioxide making up most of the other 50 percent. Certain other heterofermentative

Lactobacillus organisms are relatively inefficient in their metabolism of glucose and must derive energy from other types of organic compounds, such as galactose, malate, or fructose.

Lactobacilli are commensal inhabitants of animal and human gastrointestinal tracts, as well as the human mouth and the vagina. Commercial preparations of lactobacilli are used as probiotics to restore normal intestinal flora after the imbalance created by antibiotic therapy.

MICROCOCCUS

Micrococcus is a genus of spherical bacteria in the family Micrococcaceae that is widely disseminated in nature. Micrococci are microbiologically characterized as Gram-positive cocci, 0.5 to 3.5 µm in diameter. They are usually not pathogenic. In fact, they are normal inhabitants of the human body and may even be essential in keeping the balance among the various microbial flora of the skin. Some species are found in the dust of the air (*M. roseus*), in soil (*M. denitrificans*), in marine waters (*M. colpogenes*), and on the skin or in skin glands or skin-gland secretions of vertebrates (*M. flavus*). Those species found in milk, such as *M. luteus, M. varians*, and *M. freudenreichii*, are sometimes referred to as milk micrococci and can result in spoilage of milk products.

MYCOBACTERIUM

Mycobacterium is a genus of rod-shaped bacteria of the family Mycobacteriaceae (order Actinomycetales), the most important species of which, *M. tuberculosis* and *M. leprae*, cause tuberculosis and leprosy, respectively, in humans. *M. bovis* causes tuberculosis in cattle and in humans. Some mycobacteria are saprophytes (i.e., they live on decaying organic matter), and others are obligate parasites.

Most are found in soil and water in a free-living form or in diseased tissue of animals. Streptomycin, rifampin, and species-specific antimicrobial agents have had some success in treating *Mycobacterium* infections.

MYCOPLASMA

Mycoplasma is a genus of bacteria. The name *mycoplasma* has also been used to denote any species in the class mollicutes or any genus in the order Mycoplasmatales. Mycoplasmas are among the smallest of bacterial organisms. The cell varies from a spherical or pear shape (0.3 to 0.8 µm) to that of a slender branched filament (up to 150 µm). *Mycoplasma* species are mostly facultatively anaerobic, colonial microorganisms that lack cell walls. *Mycoplasma* species are parasites of joints and the mucous membranes lining the respiratory, genital,

PNEUMONIA

Pneumonia is an inflammation and consolidation of the lung tissue as a result of infection, inhalation of foreign particles, or irradiation. Many organisms, including viruses and fungi, can cause pneumonia, but the most common causes are bacteria, in particular species of *Streptococcus* and *Mycoplasma*. Although viral pneumonia does occur, viruses more commonly play a part in weakening the lung, thus inviting secondary pneumonia caused by bacteria. Fungal pneumonia can develop very rapidly and may be fatal, but it usually occurs in hospitalized persons who, because of impaired immunity, have reduced resistance to infection. Contaminated dusts, when inhaled by previously healthy individuals, can sometimes cause fungal lung diseases. Pneumonia can also occur as a hypersensitivity, or allergic response, to agents such as mold, humidifiers, and animal excreta or to chemical or physical injury (e.g., smoke inhalation).

Streptococcal pneumonia, caused by *Streptococcus pneumoniae*, is the single most common form of pneumonia, especially in hospitalized patients. The bacteria may live in the bodies of healthy persons and cause disease only after resistance has been lowered by other illness or infection. Viral infections such as the common cold promote streptococcal pneumonia by causing excessive

(continued on the next page)

(continued from the previous page)

secretion of fluids in the respiratory tract. These fluids provide an environment in which the bacteria flourish. Patients with bacterial pneumonia typically experience a sudden onset of high fever with chills, cough, chest pain, and difficulty in breathing. As the disease progresses, coughing becomes the major symptom. Sputum discharge may contain flecks of blood. Any chest pains result from the tenderness of the trachea (windpipe) and muscles from severe coughing.

Diagnosis usually can be established by taking a culture of the organism from the patient's sputum and by chest X-ray examination. Treatment is with specific antibiotics and supportive care, and recovery generally occurs in a few weeks. In some cases, however, the illness may become very severe, and it is sometimes fatal, particularly in elderly people and young children. Death from streptococcal pneumonia is caused by inflammation and significant and extensive bleeding in the lungs that results in the eventual cessation of breathing. Streptococcal bacteria release a toxin called pneumolysin that damages the blood vessels in the lungs, causing bleeding into the air spaces. Antibiotics may exacerbate lung damage because they are designed to kill the bacteria by breaking them open, which leads to the further release of pneumolysin. Research into the development of aerosol agents that stimulate blood clotting and that can be inhaled into the lungs and possibly be used in conjunction with traditional therapies for streptococcal pneumonia is ongoing.

Mycoplasmal pneumonia, caused by *Mycoplasma pneumoniae*, an extremely small organism, usually affects children and young adults; few cases beyond the age of 50 are seen. Most outbreaks of this disease are confined to families, small neighbourhoods, or institutions, although epidemics can occur. *M. pneumoniae* grows on the mucous membrane that lines the surfaces of internal lung structures; it does not invade the deeper tissues—muscle fibres, elastic fibres, or nerves. The bacteria can produce an oxidizing agent that might be responsible for some cell damage. Usually the organism does not invade the membrane that surrounds the lungs, but it does sometimes inflame the bronchi and alveoli.

Another bacterium, *Klebsiella pneumoniae*, although it has little ability to infect the lungs of healthy persons, produces a highly lethal pneumonia that occurs almost exclusively in hospitalized patients with impaired immunity. Other bacterial pneumonias include Legionnaire disease, caused by *Legionella pneumophilia*; pneumonia secondary to other illnesses caused by *Staphylococcus aureus* and *Hemophilus influenzae*; and psittacosis, an atypical infectious form.

or digestive tracts of ruminants, carnivores, rodents, and humans. Toxic byproducts excreted by the bacterium accumulate in the host's tissues, causing damage. *M. pneumoniae* causes a widespread but rarely fatal pneumonia in humans. *Mycoplasma* infection may also trigger a serious immune reaction in the host.

STAPHYLOCOCCUS

Staphylococcus is a genus of spherical bacteria, the best known species of which are universally present in great numbers on the mucous membranes and skin of humans and other warm-blooded animals. The term *staphylococcus*, generally used for all the species, refers to the cells' habit of aggregating in grapelike clusters. Staphylococci are microbiologically characterized as Gram-positive (in young cultures), non-spore-forming, nonmotile, facultative anaerobes.

Of significance to humans are various strains of the species *S. aureus* and *S. epidermis*. While *S. epidermis* is a mild pathogen, opportunistic only in people with lowered resistance, strains of *S. aureus* are major agents of wound infections, boils, and other human skin infections and are one of the most common causes of food poisoning.

S. aureus also causes meningitis, pneumonia, urinary tract infections, and mastitis, an infection of the breast in women or of the udder in domestic animals. In addition, local staphylococcal infections can lead to toxic shock syndrome, a disease associated with the liberation of a toxin into the bloodstream from the site of infection.

One strain that is of great concern to humans is methicillin-resistant *S. aureus* (MRSA), which is characterized by the presence of a single mutation that renders it resistant to methicillin, a semisynthetic penicillin used to treat staphylococcus infections that are resistant to mold-derived penicillin. This strain of *S. aureus* was first isolated in the early 1960s, shortly after methicillin came into wide use as an antibiotic. Today methicillin is no longer used, but the strain of MRSA to which it gave rise is commonly found on the skin, in the nose, or in the blood or urine of humans. Some 50 million people worldwide are believed to carry MRSA, which is readily passed by skin contact but rarely causes infection in healthy individuals. However, very young children and elderly or ill patients in hospitals and nursing homes are particularly susceptible to MRSA infection, which is difficult to treat because of its resistance to most antibiotics. The treatment of MRSA infections with vancomycin, an antibiotic often considered as a last line of defense against MRSA, has led to the emergence of vancomycin-resistant *S. aureus* (VRSA), against which few agents are effective. In 2005 in the United States, deaths from MRSA (approximately

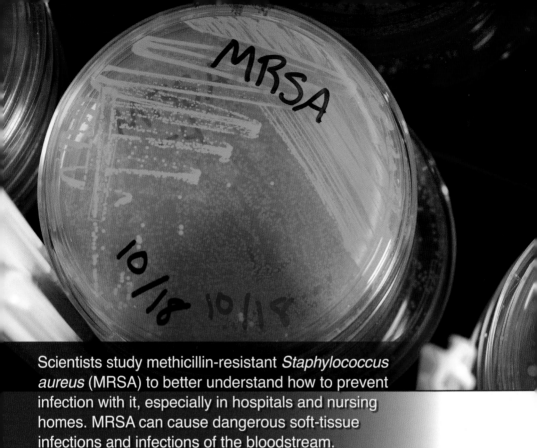

Scientists study methicillin-resistant *Staphylococcus aureus* (MRSA) to better understand how to prevent infection with it, especially in hospitals and nursing homes. MRSA can cause dangerous soft-tissue infections and infections of the bloodstream.

18,000) surpassed deaths from HIV/AIDS (approximately 17,000), underscoring the need for improved surveillance to prevent and control the spread of this potentially lethal organism. Today MRSA continues to be a problem globally, causing outbreaks of infection in places such as Asia, Australia, New Zealand, western Europe, and Latin America.

STREPTOCOCCUS

Streptococcus is a genus of spheroidal bacteria belonging to the family Streptococcaceae. The term *streptococcus* ("twisted berry") refers to the bacteria's characteristic grouping in chains that resemble a string of beads. Streptococci are microbiologically characterized as Gram-positive and nonmotile. They generally are classified by the type of carbohydrate contained in the cell wall, a system called the Lancefield classification.

Streptococcus contains a variety of species, some of which cause disease in humans and animals, while others are important in the manufacture of certain fermented products. *Streptococcus* pyogenes, often referred to as group A streptococcus bacteria, can cause rheumatic fever, impetigo, scarlet fever, puerperal fever, streptococcal toxic shock syndrome, strep throat, tonsillitis, and other upper respiratory infections. Necrotizing fasciitis, a rapidly spreading infection of the skin and underlying tissue caused by *S. pyogenes*, has been popularly referred to as the "flesh-eating disease." *Streptococcus agalactiae*, or group B streptococcus bacteria, can cause infections of the bladder and uterus in pregnant women; in newborn infants infection with the bacterium may result in sepsis (blood poisoning), meningitis (inflammation of the membranes covering the brain and spinal cord), or pneumonia. *Streptococcus pneumoniae*, also called pneumococcus, is an important human pathogen that causes pneumonia, sinusitis, otitis media, and meningitis. Fecal (enterococcal) species occur in great numbers in in the bowel and can cause urinary tract infections and endocarditis. *S. mutans*, belonging to the viridans species, inhabits the mouth and contributes to tooth decay. Among the lactic species, *S. lactis* and *S. cremoris* are used in commercial starters for the production of butter, cultured buttermilk, and certain cheeses.

STREPTOMYCES

Streptomyces is a genus of filamentous bacteria of the family Streptomycetaceae that includes more than 500 species occurring in soil and water. Many species are important in the decomposition of organic matter in soil, contributing in part to the earthy odour of soil and decaying leaves and to the fertility of soil. Certain species are noted for the production of broad-spectrum antibiotics, chemicals that the bacteria naturally produce to kill or inhibit the growth of other microorganisms.

Streptomyces are characterized as Gram-positive aerobic bacteria of complex form. They form a threadlike net called a mycelium that bears chains of spores at maturity. Their branching strands are 0.5 to 1.0 μm in diameter. The antibiotic producers include: *S. aureofaciens* (yielding chlortetracycline), *S. rimosis* (oxytetracycline), *S. griseus* (streptomycin), *S. erythraeus* (erythromycin), and *S. venezuelae* (chloramphenicol).

ARCHAEA

Domain Archaea consists of single-celled prokaryotic organisms that have distinct molecular characteristics separating them from bacteria as well as from eukaryotes. *Archaea* is derived from the Greek word *archaios*, meaning "ancient" or "primitive," and indeed some archaea exhibit characteristics worthy of that name. Members of the archaea include: *Pyrolobus fumarii*, which holds the upper temperature limit for life at 113 °C (235 °F) and was found living in hydrothermal vents; species of *Picrophilus*, which were isolated from acidic soils in Japan and are the most acid-tolerant organisms known—capable of growth at around pH 0; and the methanogens, which produce methane gas as a metabolic by-product and are found in anaerobic environments, such as in marshes, hot springs, and the guts of animals, including humans.

In some systems for classifying all of life, the archaea constitute one of three great domains of living creatures. In 1977 American microbiologist Carl Woese, on the basis of analyses of ribosomal RNA, proposed that the prokaryotes, long considered to be a single group of organisms (essentially, the bacteria), actually consist of two separate lineages. Woese called these two lineages the eubacteria and the archaebacteria. These names were subsequently changed to *bacteria* and *archaea* (the archaea being distinctly different from bacteria), but Woese's splitting of the prokaryotes into two groups has remained, and all living organisms are now considered by many biologists to fall into one of three great domains: Archaea, Bacteria, and Eukarya. Further molecular analysis has shown that domain Archaea consists of two major subdivisions, the Crenarchaeota and the Euryarchaeota, and two minor ancient lineages, the Korarchaeota and the Nanoarchaeota.

HABITATS

Archaea are microorganisms that define the limits of life on Earth. They were originally discovered and described in extreme environments, such as hydrothermal vents and terrestrial hot springs. They were also found in a diverse range of highly saline, acidic, and anaerobic environments.

Although many of the cultured archaea are extremophiles, these organisms in their respective extreme habitats represent only a minority of the total diversity of the Archaea domain. The majority of archaea cannot be cultured within the laboratory setting, and their ubiquitous presence in global habitats has been realized through the use of culture-independent techniques. One commonly used culture-independent technique is the isolation and analysis of nucleic acids (i.e., DNA and RNA) directly from an environment, rather than the analysis of cultured samples isolated from the same environment. Culture-independent studies have shown that archaea are abundant and fulfill important ecological roles in cold and temperate ecosystems. Uncultivated organisms in the subdivision Crenarchaeota are postulated to be the most abundant ammonia-oxidizing organisms in soils and to account for a large proportion (roughly 20 percent) of the microorganisms present in the picoplankton in the world's oceans. In the subdivision Euryarchaeota, uncultivated organisms in deep-sea marine sediments are responsible for the removal of methane, a potent greenhouse gas, via anaerobic oxidation of methane stored in these sediments. In contrast, uncultivated methanogenic (methane-producing) euryarchaea from terrestrial anaerobic environments, such as rice fields, are estimated to generate approximately 10–25 percent of global methane emissions.

The cultured representatives of the Crenarchaeota are from high-temperature environments, such as hot springs and submarine hydrothermal vents. Likewise, cultured members of the Euryarchaeota include organisms isolated from hot environments, organisms that are methanogenic, and organisms that grow vigorously in high-salt environments (halophiles). Organisms in the lineages Korarchaeota and Nanoarchaeota also inhabit high-temperature environments; however, the nanoarchaea are highly unusual because they grow and divide on the surface of another archaea, *Ignicoccus*. Nanoarchaea, which were discovered in 2002, contain both the smallest known living cell (1/100th the size of *Escherichia coli*) and the smallest known genome (480 kilobases [1 kilobase = 1,000 base pairs of DNA]; for comparison, the human genome contains 3 million kilobases). Members of the Korarchaeota and Nanoarchaeota have not been detected in pure culture; rather, they have been detected only in mixed laboratory cultures.

Archaea are also found living in association with eukaryotes; for example, methanogenic archaea are present in the digestive systems of some animals, including humans. Some archaea also form symbiotic relationships with sponges; in fact, *Cenarchaeum symbiosum* was grown in the laboratory with its host sponge and was the first nonthermophilic Crenarchaeota to be cultured and described.

FEATURES

Although the domains Bacteria, Archaea, and Eukarya were founded on genetic criteria, biochemical properties also indicate that the archaea form an independent group within the prokaryotes and that they share traits with both the bacteria and the eukaryotes. Major examples of these traits include:

1. **Cell walls:** Virtually all bacteria contain peptidoglycan in their cell walls; however,

archaea and eukaryotes lack peptidoglycan. Various types of cell walls exist in the
archaea. Therefore, the absence or presence of peptidoglycan is a distinguishing
feature between the archaea and bacteria.

2. **Fatty acids:** Bacteria and eukaryotes produce membrane lipids consisting of fatty
acids linked by ester bonds to a molecule of
glycerol. In contrast, the archaea have ether
bonds connecting fatty acids to molecules
of glycerol. Although a few bacteria also
contain ether-linked lipids, no archaea
have been discovered that contain ester-
linked lipids.

3. **Complexity of RNA polymerase:** Transcription within all types of organisms is
performed by an enzyme called RNA polymerase, which copies a DNA template into
an RNA product. Bacteria contain a simple
RNA polymerase consisting of four polypeptides. However, both archaea and eukaryotes have multiple RNA polymerases that
contain multiple polypeptides. For example,
the RNA polymerases of archaea contain
more than eight polypeptides. The RNA
polymerases of eukaryotes also consist of
a high number of polypeptides (10–12), with
the relative sizes of the polypeptides being
similar to that of hyperthermophilic archaeal

RNA polymerase. Therefore, the archaeal RNA polymerases more closely resemble RNA polymerases of eukaryotes rather than those of bacteria.

4. **Protein synthesis:** Various features of protein synthesis in the archaea are similar to those of eukaryotes but not of bacteria. A prominent difference is that bacteria have an initiator tRNA (transfer RNA) that has a modified methionine, whereas eukaryotes and archaea have an initiator tRNA with an unmodified methionine.

5. **Metabolism:** Various types of metabolism exist in both archaea and bacteria that do not exist in eukaryotes, including nitrogen fixation, denitrification, chemolithotrophy, and hyperthermophilic growth. Methanogenesis (the production of methane as a metabolic by-product) occurs only in the domain Archaea, specifically in the subdivision Euryarchaeota. Classical photosynthesis using chlorophyll has not been found in any archaea.

EXTREMOPHILES

Extremophiles are organisms that are tolerant to environmental extremes and that have evolved to grow optimally under one or more of these extreme conditions, hence the suffix *phile*, meaning "one who loves." Extremophilic organisms are primarily prokaryotic (archaea and bacteria), with few eukaryotic examples.

Extremophiles are defined by the environmental conditions in which they grow optimally. The organisms may be described as acidophilic (optimal growth between pH 1 and pH 5); alkaliphilic (optimal growth above pH 9); halophilic (optimal growth

Researchers who work with extremophiles that are active at cold temperatures have to keep the samples in sub-zero temperatures.

in environments with high concentrations of salt); thermophilic (optimal growth between 60 and 80 °C [140 and 176 °F]); hyperthermophilic (optimal growth above 80 °C [176 °F]); psychrophilic (optimal growth at 15 °C [60 °F] or lower, with a maximum tolerant temperature of 20 °C [68 °F] and minimal growth at or below 0 °C [32 °F]); piezophilic, or barophilic (optimal growth at high hydrostatic pressure); oligotrophic (growth in nutritionally limited environments); endolithic (growth within rock or within pores of mineral grains); and xerophilic (growth in dry conditions, with low water availability). Some extremophiles are adapted simultaneously to multiple stresses (polyextremophile); common examples include thermoacidophiles and haloalkaliphiles.

Extremophiles are of biotechnological interest, as they produce extremozymes, defined as enzymes that are functional under extreme conditions. Extremozymes are useful in industrial production procedures and research applications because of their ability to remain active under the severe conditions (e.g., high temperature, pressure, and pH) typically employed in these processes.

The study of extremophiles provides an understanding of the physicochemical parameters defining life on Earth and may provide insight into how life on Earth originated. The postulations that extreme environmental conditions existed on primitive Earth and that life arose in hot environments have led to the theory that extremophiles are vestiges of primordial organisms and thus are models of ancient life.

Extremophiles are also of research importance in the field of astrobiology. Extremophiles that are active at cold temperatures are of particular interest in this field, as the majority of the bodies in the solar system are frozen. Understanding the limits of life on Earth provides scientists with information about the possible existence of extraterrestrial life and with clues about where and how to search for life on other solar bodies.

CHAPTER 4

FEATURES AND EVOLUTION OF VIRUSES

V iruses occupy a special taxonomic position: they are not plants, animals, or prokaryotic bacteria (single-cell organisms without defined nuclei), and they are generally placed in their own kingdom. In fact, viruses should not even be considered organisms, in the strictest sense, because they are not free-living; i.e., they cannot reproduce and carry on metabolic processes without a host cell.

All true viruses contain nucleic acid—either DNA (deoxyribonucleic acid) or RNA (ribonucleic acid)—and protein. The nucleic acid encodes the genetic information unique for each virus. The infective, extracellular (outside the cell) form of a virus is called the virion. It contains at least one unique protein synthesized by specific genes in the nucleic acid of that virus. In virtually all viruses, at least one of these proteins forms a shell (called a capsid) around the nucleic acid. Certain viruses also have other proteins internal to the capsid; some of these proteins act as enzymes, often during the synthesis of viral nucleic acids. Viroids (meaning "viruslike") are disease-causing organisms that contain only nucleic acid and have no structural proteins. Other viruslike particles called prions are composed primarily of a protein tightly complexed with a small nucleic acid molecule. Prions are very resistant to inactivation

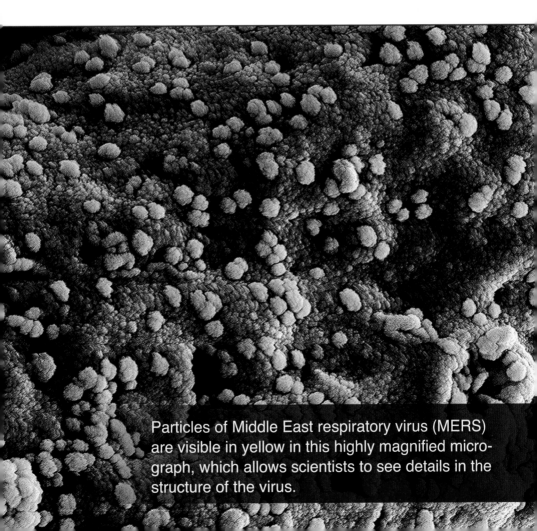

Particles of Middle East respiratory virus (MERS) are visible in yellow in this highly magnified micrograph, which allows scientists to see details in the structure of the virus.

and appear to cause degenerative brain disease in mammals, including humans.

Viruses are quintessential parasites; they depend on the host cell for almost all of their life-sustaining functions. Unlike true organisms, viruses cannot synthesize proteins, because they lack ribosomes (cell organelles) for the translation of viral messenger RNA (mRNA; a complementary copy of the nucleic acid of the nucleus that associates with ribosomes and directs protein synthesis) into proteins. Viruses must use the ribosomes of their host cells to translate viral mRNA into viral proteins.

Viruses are also energy parasites; unlike cells, they cannot generate or store energy in the form of adenosine triphosphate (ATP). The virus derives energy, as well as all other metabolic functions, from the host cell. The invading virus uses the nucleotides and amino acids of the host cell to synthesize its nucleic acids and proteins, respectively. Some viruses use the lipids and sugar chains of the host cell to form their membranes and glycoproteins (proteins linked to short polymers consisting of several sugars).

The true infectious part of any virus is its nucleic acid, either DNA or RNA, but never both. In many viruses, but not all, the nucleic acid alone, stripped of its capsid, can infect (transfect) cells, although considerably less efficiently than can the intact virions. The virion capsid has three functions: (1) to protect the viral nucleic acid from digestion by certain enzymes (nucleases), (2) to furnish sites on its surface that recognize and attach (adsorb) the virion to receptors on the surface of the host cell, and, in some viruses, (3) to provide proteins that form part of a specialized component which enables the virion to penetrate through the cell surface membrane or, in special cases, to inject the infectious nucleic acid into the interior of the host cell.

HOST RANGE AND DISTRIBUTION

Logic originally dictated that viruses be identified on the basis of the host they infect. This is justified in many cases, but not in others, and the host range and distribution of viruses are only one criterion for their classification. It is still traditional to divide viruses into three categories: those that infect animals, plants, or bacteria.

Virtually all plant viruses are transmitted by insects or other organisms (vectors) that feed on plants. The hosts of animal viruses vary from protozoans (single-celled animal organisms) to humans. Many viruses infect either invertebrate animals or vertebrates, and some infect both. Certain viruses that cause serious diseases of animals and humans are carried by arthropods. These vector-borne

DISCOVERING VIRUSES

Russian microbiologist Dmitry Iosifovich Ivanovsky (1894–1920), from his study of mosaic disease in tobacco, was one of the first scientists to describe many of the characteristics of the entities that came to be known as viruses. Although he is generally credited as the discoverer of viruses, they were also independently discovered and named by the Dutch botanist Martinus W. Beijerinck only a few years later.

While a student at St. Petersburg University, Ivanovsky was asked in 1887 to investigate "wildfire," a disease that was infecting tobacco plantations of the Ukraine and Bessarabia. In 1890 he was commissioned to study a different disease that was destroying tobacco plants in the Crimea. He determined that the infection was mosaic disease, which was believed at the time to be caused by bacteria. Using a filtering method for the isolation of bacteria, Ivanovsky discovered that filtered sap from diseased plants could transfer the infection to healthy plants. Further researches led Ivanovsky to conclude that the causal agent was an exceedingly small parasitic microorganism that was invisible even under great magnification and that could permeate porcelain filters designed to trap ordinary bacteria. He differed from later researchers of viruses only in his supposition that the pathogenic agent in question was a minuscule bacterium, rather than an entirely new and different type of agent. He published his findings in an article, "On Two Diseases of Tobacco" (1892), and a dissertation, *Mosaic Disease in Tobacco* (1902).

Martinus W. Beijerinck (1851–1931), who founded the discipline of virology, was the first to recognize that viruses are reproducing entities that are different from other organisms. He also discovered new types of bacteria from soil and described biological nitrogen fixation (the conversion of nitrogen gas into ammonium, a form usable by plants). Beijerinck embraced dispute and at times showed little respect for the work of others, on one occasion turning down a visit to the laboratory of German bacteriologist Robert Koch, thinking he had little to learn from Koch. Perhaps for these reasons, as well as his distaste for medical bacteriology and his focus on soil and plant microorganisms, his work was not as widely celebrated as that of Koch and French chemist and microbiologist Louis Pasteur.

viruses multiply in both the invertebrate vector and the vertebrate host.

Certain viruses are limited in their host range to the various orders of vertebrates. Some viruses appear to be adapted for growth only in ectothermic vertebrates (animals commonly referred to as cold-blooded, such as fishes and reptiles), possibly because they can only reproduce at low temperatures. Other viruses are limited in their host range to endothermic vertebrates (animals commonly referred to as warm-blooded, such as mammals).

SIZE AND SHAPE

The amount and arrangement of the proteins and nucleic acid of viruses determine their size and shape. The nucleic acid and proteins of each class of viruses assemble themselves into a structure called a nucleoprotein, or nucleocapsid. Some viruses have more than one layer of protein surrounding the nucleic acid; still others have a lipoprotein membrane (called an envelope), derived from the membrane of the host cell, that surrounds the nucleocapsid core. Penetrating the membrane are additional proteins that determine the specificity of the virus to host cells. The protein and nucleic acid constituents have properties unique for each class of virus; when assembled, they determine the size and shape of the virus for that specific class.

Viruses vary in diameter from 20 nanometres (nm; 1 nm = 3.9×10^{-8} inch) to 250–400 nm. Only the largest and most complex viruses can be seen under the light microscope at the highest resolution. Any determination of the size of a virus also must take into account its shape, since different classes of viruses have distinctive shapes.

Shapes of viruses are predominantly of two kinds: rods, or filaments, so called because of the linear array of the nucleic acid and the protein subunits; and spheres, which are actually 20-sided (icosahedral) polygons. Most plant viruses are small and are either filaments or polygons, as are many bacterial viruses. The larger and more-complex bacteriophages, however, contain as their genetic information double-stranded DNA and combine both filamentous and polygonal shapes. The classic T4 bacteriophage is composed of a polygonal head, which contains the DNA genome and a special-function rod-shaped tail of long fibres. Structures such as these are unique to the bacteriophages.

Animal viruses exhibit extreme variation in size and shape. The smallest animal viruses belong to the families Parvoviridae and Picornaviridae and measure about 20 nm and about 30 nm in diameter, respectively. Viruses of these two families are icosahedrons and contain nucleic acids with limited genetic information. Viruses of the family Poxviridae are about 250 to 400 nm in their longest dimension, and they are neither polygons nor filaments.

Poxviruses are structurally more complex than simple bacteria, despite their close resemblance. Animal viruses that have rod-shaped (helical) nucleocapsids are those enclosed in an envelope; these viruses are found in the families Paramyxoviridae, Orthomyxoviridae, Coronaviridae, and Rhabdoviridae. Not all enveloped viruses contain helical nucleocapsids, however; those of the families Herpesviridae, Retroviridae, and Togaviridae have polygonal nucleocapsids. Most enveloped viruses appear to be spherical, although the rhabdoviruses are elongated cylinders.

The criteria used for classifying viruses into families and genera are primarily based on three structural considerations: (1) the type and size of their nucleic acid, (2) the shape and size of the capsids, and (3) the presence of a lipid envelope, derived from the host cell, surrounding the viral nucleocapsid.

NUCLEIC ACID

As is true in all forms of life, the nucleic acid of each virus encodes the genetic information for the synthesis of all proteins. In almost all free-living organisms, the genetic information is in the form of double-stranded DNA arranged as a spiral lattice joined at the bases along the length of the molecule (a double helix). In viruses, however, genetic information can come in a variety of forms, including single-stranded or double-stranded DNA or RNA.

The nucleic acids of virions are arranged into genomes. All double-stranded DNA viruses consist of a single large molecule, whereas most double-stranded RNA viruses have segmented genomes, with each segment usually representing a single gene that encodes the information for synthesizing a single protein. Viruses with single-stranded genomic DNA are usually small, with limited genetic information. Some single-stranded DNA viruses are composed of two populations of virions, each consisting of complementary single-stranded DNA of polarity opposite to that of the other.

The virions of most plant viruses and many animal and bacterial viruses are composed of single-stranded RNA. In most of these viruses, the genomic RNA is termed a positive strand because the genomic RNA acts as mRNA for direct synthesis (translation) of viral protein. Several large families of animal viruses, and one that includes both plant and animal viruses (the Rhabdoviridae), however, contain genomic single-stranded RNA, termed a negative strand, which is complementary to mRNA. All of these negative-strand RNA viruses have an enzyme, called an RNA-dependent RNA polymerase (tran-scriptase), which must first catalyze the synthesis of complementary mRNA from the virion genomic RNA before viral protein synthesis can occur. These varia-tions in the nucleic acids of viruses form one central criterion for classification of all viruses. A distinctive large family of single-stranded RNA viruses is called Retroviridae; the RNA of these viruses is positive, but the viruses are equipped with an enzyme, called a reverse transcriptase, that copies the single-stranded RNA to form double-stranded DNA.

PROTEIN CAPSID

The protein capsid provides the second major cri-terion for the classification of viruses. The capsid surrounds the virus and is composed of a finite number of protein subunits known as capsomeres, which usually associate with, or are found close to, the virion nucleic acid.

There are two major classes of viruses based on the protein capsid: (1) those in which a single (or segmented) linear nucleic acid molecule with two free ends is essentially completely extended or somewhat coiled (a helix) and (2) those in which the nucleic acid, which may or may not be a covalently closed circle, is wound tightly into a condensed configuration, like a ball of yarn. These two classes of virus assume in the first case a long, extended rod-like structure and in the second case a symmetrical polygon.

By far the best-studied example of a helical rod-shaped virus is the tobacco mosaic virus, which was crystallized by Wendell Stanley in 1935. The tobacco mosaic virus contains a genome of single-stranded RNA encased by 2,130 molecules of a single protein; there are 161/3 protein molecules for each turn of the RNA helix in the ratio of three nucleotides for each protein molecule.

Under the right environmental conditions, viral RNA and protein molecules in liquid suspension will assemble themselves into a perfectly formed and fully infectious virus. The length of the helical virus capsid is determined by the length of the nucleic acid molecule, which is the framework for the

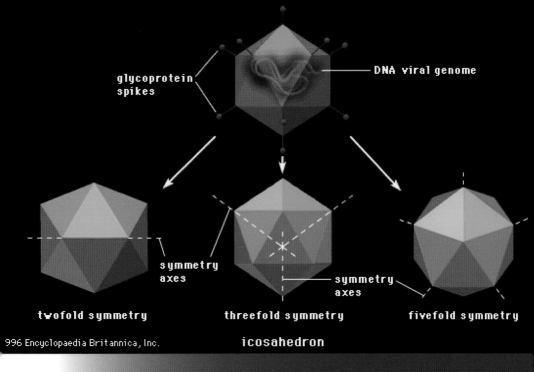

icosahedron

A virus icosahedron (20-sided structure) shown on the (*left*) twofold, (*centre*) threefold, and (*right*) fivefold axes of symmetry. Edges of the upper and lower surfaces are drawn in solid and broken lines, respectively.

assembly of the capsid protein. The various helical viruses have different lengths and widths depending on the size of the nucleic acid as well as on the mass and shape of the protein molecule. Some of these helical viruses form rigid rods, while others form flexible rods, depending on the properties of the assembled proteins.

Polygonal viruses vary greatly in size, from 20 to 150 nm in diameter, essentially proportional to the size of the nucleic acid molecule coiled up inside the virion. Most, if not all, of the polygonal viruses are icosahedral; like a geodesic dome, they are formed by equilateral triangles, in this case 20. Each triangle is composed of protein subunits (capsomeres), often in the form of hexons (multiples of six) that are the building blocks of the capsid. There are 12 vertices (the apical junctions of these 20 triangles), each comprising a penton (five subunits). These icosahedral virions have three axes of fivefold, threefold, and twofold rotational symmetry. The number of capsomeres is a basis for taxonomic classification of these virus families. Certain icosahedral viruses, usually those that are more complex, contain internal proteins adhering to the nucleic acid that are not accessible at the surface of the virions.

LIPOPROTEIN ENVELOPE

Surrounding viruses of either helical or icosahedral symmetry are lipoprotein envelopes, unit membranes of two lipid layers interspersed with protein molecules (lipoprotein bilayer). These viral membranes are composed of phospholipids and neutral lipids (largely cholesterol) derived from cell membranes during the process known as budding. Virtually all proteins of the cell membrane, however, are replaced by proteins of viral origin during budding. Although all the viral envelope lipids originate from the cell, their relative proportions vary from those in the cell membrane because the viral proteins select only certain lipids during budding.

Associated with the virion membrane are "integral" glycoproteins, which completely traverse the lipid bilayer, and "peripheral" matrix proteins, which line the inner surface. The glycoproteins contain regions of amino acids that, in the first step of viral infection, recognize host-cell receptors. Matrix proteins appear to function in the selection of regions of the cell membrane to be used for the viral membrane, as well as to aid the virion in entering cells.

EVOLUTION

Owing to their simplicity, viruses were at first considered to be the primordial life-forms. This concept is almost certainly incorrect because viruses are completely devoid of the machinery for life processes; therefore, they could not have survived in the absence of cells. Viruses probably evolved from cells rather than cells from viruses. It seems likely that all viruses trace their origins to cellular genes and can be considered as pieces of rogue nucleic acids. Although it is easier to imagine the cellular origin of DNA viruses than RNA viruses, the RNA viruses conceivably could have had their origins from cellular RNA transcripts made from cellular DNA. In fact, the discovery that many cells contain reverse transcriptase capable of converting RNA to DNA seems to suggest that conversion of RNA to DNA and DNA to RNA is not rare. Indeed, some speculate that RNA is the primordial genetic information from which DNA evolved to produce more-complex life-forms.

Other possible progenitors of viruses are the plasmids (small circular DNA molecules independent of chromosomes), which are more readily transferred from cell to cell than are chromosomes. Theoretically, plasmids could have acquired capsid genes, which coded for proteins to coat the plasmid DNA, converting it into a virus. In brief, it is likely that viruses originated from the degradation of cellular nucleic acids, which acquired the property of being readily transferable from cell to cell during the process of evolution. The fact that normal proto-oncogenes of a cell have nucleic acid sequences that are almost identical to the oncogenes of retroviruses lends credence to the theory that viruses originated from cellular genes.

Viruses that infect animals can jump from one species to another, causing a new, usually severe disease in the new host. For example, a virus in the Coronaviridae family jumped from an animal reservoir, believed to be horseshoe bats, to humans, causing a highly pathogenic disease in humans called severe acute respiratory syndrome (SARS). The ability of the SARS coronavirus to jump from horseshoe bats to humans undoubtedly required genetic changes in the virus. The changes are suspected to have occurred in the palm civet since the

Airports like this one in Kuala Lumpur, Malaysia, had to screen travelers for SARS during the 2002–03 outbreak that killed almost 800 people, according to the World Health Organization.

SARS virus present in horseshoe bats is unable to infect humans directly.

Influenza A viruses that infect humans can undergo a dramatic antigenic change, called antigenic shift, which generates viruses that cause pandemics. This dramatic change occurs because influenza A viruses have a large animal reservoir, wild aquatic birds. The RNA genome of influenza A viruses is in the form of eight segments. If an intermediate host, probably the pig, is simultaneously infected with a human and avian influenza A virus, the genome RNA segments can be reassorted, yielding a new virus that has a surface protein that is immunologically distinct from that of influenza A viruses that have been circulating in the human population. Because the human population will have little or no immunological protection against the new virus, a pandemic will result. This is what most likely occurred in the Asian flu pandemic of 1957 and the Hong Kong flu pandemic of 1968.

Pandemic influenza A viruses can also apparently arise by a different mechanism. It has been postulated that the strain that caused the influenza pandemic of 1918–19 derived all eight RNA segments from an avian virus and that this virus then underwent multiple mutations in the process of adapting to mammalian cells. The bird flu viruses, which have spread from Asia to Europe and Africa since the 1990s, appear to be taking this route to pandemic capability. These viruses, which have been directly transmitted from chickens to humans, contain only avian genes and are highly pathogenic in humans, causing a mortality rate higher than 50 percent. Bird flu viruses have not yet acquired the ability to transmit efficiently from humans to humans, and it is not known what genetic changes must take place for them to do so.

The cycles and patterns of viral infection vary depending on the type of virus involved. In order to replicate, however, all viruses must first find a suitable host cell. Whereas some viruses then lie dormant for an indefinite period of time, others set to work appropriating the cells' genetic replication machinery. The latter is accomplished primarily through the ability of a virus to integrate into host cell DNA. The subsequent manipulation of the host's genetic machinery results in the generation of numerous viral progeny. When the host cell dies, the progeny are freed to infect new host cells, repeating the infection and replication cycle. The mechanisms of viral infection sometimes involve phenomena such as lysogeny, in which a bacteriophage lies dormant within a host bacterial cell and eventually awakens, replicates, and causes the cell to break open (lyse), and malignant transformation, in which animal cells infected with certain viruses are transformed into cancer cells. In addition to cancer, viral infections in humans also underlie various other diseases, ranging from gastrointestinal illness to influenza to AIDS. Thus, the development of vaccines to prevent infection and of antiviral drugs to treat infection form important areas of research at the crossroads of virology and medicine.

THE CYCLE OF INFECTION

Viruses can reproduce only within a host cell. The parental virus (virion) gives rise to numerous progeny, usually genetically and structurally identical to the parent virus. The actions of the virus depend both on its destructive tendencies toward a specific host cell and on environmental conditions. In the vegetative cycle of viral infection, multiplication of progeny viruses can be rapid. This cycle of infection often results in the death of the cell and the release of many virus progeny. Certain viruses, particularly bacteriophages, are called temperate (or latent) because the infection does not immediately result in cell death. The viral genetic material remains dormant or is actually integrated into the genome of the host cell. Cells infected with temperate viruses are called lysogenic because the cells tend to be broken down when they encounter some chemical

viruses

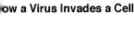

body cell

1. A virus enters a cell.

2. Substances in the cell begin to strip off the virus's outer coat of protein.

3. The nucleic acid in the center of the virus is released.

4. The nucleic acid gets into the cell's chemical manufacturing system.

5. The cell "ignores" its own chemical needs and switches to making new viruses.

6. The cell is sometimes destroyed in the process. Many of the new viruses are released to infect other cells.

The process by which a virus invades a cell and reproduces.

or physical factor, such as ultraviolet light. In addition, many animal and plant viruses, the genetic information of which is not integrated into the host DNA, may lie dormant in tissues for long periods of time without causing much, if any, tissue damage. Viral infection does not always result in cell death or tissue injury; in fact, most viruses lie dormant in tissue without ever causing pathological effects, or they do so only under other, often environmental, provocations.

Although the reproductive pathways of different viruses vary considerably, there are certain basic principles and a particular series of events in the cycle of infection for most, if not all, viruses. The first step in the cycle of infection is that the invading parental virus (virion) must attach to the surface of the host cell (adsorption). In the second step, the intact virion either penetrates the outer membrane and enters the cell's interior (cytoplasm), or it injects the genetic material of the virus into the interior of the cell while the protein capsid (and envelope, if present) remains at the cell surface. In the case of whole-virion penetration, a subsequent process (uncoating) liberates the genetic material from the capsid and envelope, if present. In either case, the viral genetic material cannot begin to synthesize protein until it emerges from the capsid or envelope.

Certain bacterial viruses, such as the T4 bacteriophage, have evolved an elaborate process of infection: following adsorption and firm attachment of the virus's tail to the bacterium surface by means of proteinaceous "pins," the muscle-like tail contracts, and the tail plug penetrates the cell wall and underlying membrane and injects virus (phage) DNA into the cell. Other bacteriophages penetrate the cell membrane by different means, such as injecting the nucleic acid through the male (sex) pili of the bacterium. In all bacterial viruses, penetration transmits the viral nucleic acid through a rigid bacterial cell wall.

Plant cells also have rigid cell walls, which plant viruses cannot ordinarily penetrate. Plant viruses, however, have not evolved their own systems for injecting nucleic acids into host cells, and so they are transmitted by the proboscis of insects that feed on plants. In the laboratory, plant viruses penetrate plant cells if the cell walls have been abraded with sandpaper or if cell protoplasts (plasma membrane, cytoplasm, and nucleus) are devoid of walls.

Penetration of animal cells by viruses involves different processes, because animal cells are enclosed not by walls but by a flexible lipoprotein bilayer membrane. Most animal viruses, whether or not they are encased in lipid envelopes, penetrate cells in an intact form by a process called endocytosis. The membrane invaginates and engulfs a virus particle adsorbed to a cell, usually in an area of the membrane called a coated pit, which is lined by a special protein known as clathrin. As the coated pit invaginates, it is pinched off in the cytoplasm to form a coated vesicle. The coated vesicle fuses with cytoplasmic endosomes (membrane-enclosed vesicles) and then with cell organelles called lysosomes, which are membrane-enclosed vesicles containing enzymes. In an acidic environment, the membrane of an enveloped virus fuses with the endosome membrane, and the viral nucleocapsid is released into the cytoplasm. Nonenveloped viruses presumably undergo a similar process, by which the protein capsid is degraded, releasing the naked viral nucleic acid into the cytoplasm.

The order of the stages of viral replication that follows the uncoating of the genome varies for different virus classes. For many virus families

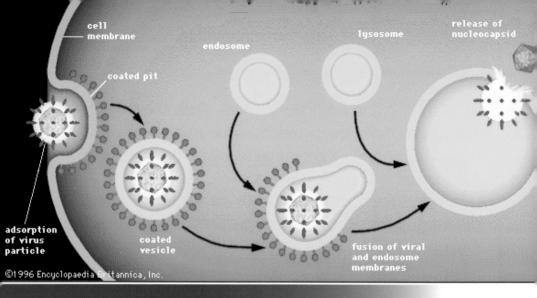

Adsorption to and entry into a cell of an enveloped animal virus by the process of endocytosis into clathrin-coated vesicles, which fuse with large vesicles (endosomes and lysosomes). The process triggered by the viral glycoprotein results in fusion and release of the viral nucleocapsid into the cytoplasm.

the third step in the cycle of infection is transcription of the genome of the virus to produce viral mRNA, followed by the fourth step, translation of viral mRNA into proteins. For those viruses in which the genomic nucleic acid is an RNA that can serve as a messenger (i.e., positive-strand RNA viruses), the third step is the translation of the RNA to form viral proteins; some of these newly synthesized viral proteins are enzymes that synthesize nucleic acids (polymerases), which carry out a fourth step, the transcription of more mRNA from the viral genome. For the more complicated DNA viruses, such as adenoviruses and herpesviruses, some regions of the genome synthesize "early" mRNAs, which are translated into polymerases that initiate the transcription of "late" regions of the DNA into mRNAs, which are then translated into structural proteins.

Regardless of how the third and fourth steps proceed, the fifth step in the cycle of infection is replication (reproduction of the parental genome to make progeny genomes). The sixth step is the assembly of the newly replicated progeny genomes with structural proteins to make fully formed progeny virions. The seventh and last step is the release of progeny virions by lysis of the host cell through the process of either extrusion or budding, depending on the nature of the virus. In a host animal or cell culture, this seven-step process may be repeated many times; the progeny virions released from the original site of infection are then transmitted to other sites or to other individuals.

For most animal and plant RNA viruses, all replicative events take place in the cytoplasm; in fact, many of these RNA viruses can grow in host cells in which the nucleus has been removed. Replication of most animal and plant DNA viruses, as well as the RNA influenza virus, takes place in the nucleus. In these viruses, transcription takes place in the nucleus, the mRNA migrates to the cytoplasm where it is translated, and these viral proteins migrate back to the nucleus, where they assemble with newly replicated progeny genomes. Migration of newly translated viral proteins from the cytoplasm to the nucleus is generally a function of specific amino acid sequences called "signals," which translocate the protein through pores in the nucleus membrane.

INTEGRATION OF THE VIRUS INTO THE HOST DNA

Viral integration into host cell DNA enables viruses to replicate themselves using the host's own cellular components. For the virus, this represents a very efficient mode of replication, but for the host cell, there can occur any of a variety of consequences. Although viral DNA integration often leads to death of the host cell, in some instances viral genes remain integrated in the host DNA throughout multiple host-cell division cycles. The viral genes may give the host cell new characteristics, such as the ability to cause disease (in the case of infected, normally nonpathogenic bacterial cells) or the ability to replicate indefinitely (in the case of infected animal cells). The acquisition of such properties stems from the integration phenomena of lysogeny and malignant transformation.

LYSOGENY

Many bacterial and animal viruses lie dormant in the infected cell, and their DNA may be integrated into the DNA of the host cell chromosome. The integrated viral DNA replicates as the cell genome replicates; after cell division, the integrated viral DNA is duplicated and usually distributed equally to the two cells that result. The bacteria that carry the noninfective precursor phage, called the prophage, remain healthy and continue to grow until they are stimulated by some perturbing factor, such as ultraviolet light. The prophage DNA is then excised from the bacterial chromosome, and the phage replicates, producing many progeny phages and lysing the host bacterial cell. This process, originally discovered in temperate bacteriophages in 1950 by the French microbiologist André Lwoff, is called lysogeny.

The classic example of a temperate bacteriophage is called lambda (λ) virus, which readily causes lysogeny in certain species of the bacterium *Escherichia coli*. The DNA of the λ bacteriophage is integrated into the DNA of the *E. coli* host chromosome at specific regions called attachment sites. The integrated prophage is the inherited, noninfectious form of the virus; it contains a gene that represses the lytic functions of the phage and thus assures that the host cell will continue to replicate the phage DNA along with its own and that it will not be destroyed by the virus. Ultraviolet light, or other factors that stimulate the replication of DNA in the host cell, causes the formation of a recAprotease, an enzyme that breaks apart the λ phage repressor and induces λ phage replication and, eventually, destruction of the host cell.

Excision of the prophage DNA from the host chromosomal DNA (as an initial step in the synthesis of an infective, lytic virus) sometimes results in the removal of some of the host cell DNA, which is packaged into defective bacteriophages; part of the bacteriophage DNA is removed and replaced at the other end by a gene of the host bacterium. Such a virus particle is called a transducing phage because, when it infects a bacterial cell, it can transmit the gene captured by λ phage DNA into the next bacterial cell it infects. Transduction by bacteriophages is an efficient means for transferring the genetic information of one bacterial cell to another.

This means of transferring genetic information, called lysogenic conversion, imparts genes with special functions to bacterial cells without such functions. It is common in bacteria and is an important aspect of the epidemiology (incidence, distribution, and control) of infectious diseases. For example, the bacterium *Corynebacterium diphtheriae* is the causative agent of diphtheria, but only when it contains the prophage of bacteriophage β, which codes for the toxin that is responsible for the disease.

MALIGNANT TRANSFORMATION

A phenomenon analogous to bacterial cell lysogeny occurs in animal cells infected with certain viruses. These animal viruses do not generally cause disease immediately for certain animal cells. Instead, animal cells are persistently infected with such viruses, the DNA of which (provirus) is integrated into the chromosomal DNA of the host cell. In general, cells with integrated proviral DNA are converted into cancer cells, a phenomenon known as malignant transformation. As is the case with bacterial prophages, the transformed animal cell contains no infectious virus but only the integrated provirus DNA, which replicates along with the dividing cell's chromosomes. Therefore, following mitosis of the transformed cell, each new cell receives a copy of the proviral DNA. The hallmark of these transformed animal cells is that their growth is uncontrollable; unlike normal cells, their growth is not inhibited by contact with other cells, and they lose their capacity to adhere (anchor) to certain surfaces. Growth of normal tissues and organs is also controlled by a genetic phenomenon called programmed cell death, or apoptosis, in which a certain number of cells will die and be eliminated after a finite number of divisions. Malignant transformation can impede programmed cell death, thus allowing the cells to grow uncontrolled, resulting in cancer.

Among the animal viruses that cause malignant transformation by integration of proviral DNA are several families of DNA viruses and one large family of RNA viruses, the Retroviridae. Viruses of the family Polyomaviridae, a group of papovaviruses, were perhaps the first to be associated with malignancy (causing death or illness) in animals. Polyomavirus is widespread in mice; it can infect other rodents, and it can cause tumours in infected animals. Another virus of the family Polyomaviridae is simian virus 40 (SV40), originally isolated from cells of the African green monkey (*Cercopithecus sabaeus*), where it grows rapidly and kills the cells. Infection of rodent or human cells, however, results in an abortive infection (an incompatibility between the virus and the host cell) but sometimes induces malignancy (sarcomas or lymphomas) in the occasional cell that is transformed. Viruses related to polyomavirus and SV40 have been isolated from humans, one of which, the JC virus, appears to be the causative agent of a fatal neurological disease called progressive multifocal leukoencephalopathy. In general, however, the human polyomaviruses are not clearly associated with disease.

Other papovaviruses include the papillomaviruses (family Papillomaviridae), which are also small polygonal viruses containing circular double-stranded DNA. The papillomaviruses are associated with usually benign (nonthreatening)

but widespread tumours, called papillomas or pol-
yps, occurring in human skin and the genital tract.
Specific papillomaviruses have been identified in
humans in common warts and in genital warts (condylomata acuminata). Cancers of the human genital
tract, particularly uterine cancer of the cervix, are
frequently found in association with human papillomavirus type 16 (HPV 16); the virus undoubtedly is
transmitted as a venereal disease.

Certain viruses of the family Adenoviridae, originally found in the tonsils and adenoids of humans,
cause malignant transformation in certain cells. This
phenomenon of cancer induction under laboratory
conditions has been studied widely, but there is no
evidence that the common adenoviruses cause cancers in humans. The common viruses of the family Herpesviridae, however, including the common
herpes simplex viruses that cause cold sores and
the venereal disease genital herpes, are suspected
of being causative agents of cancer. Like the adenoviruses, the herpesviruses can cause malignant
transformations, and their DNA is integrated into the
host cell chromosome. A herpesvirus known as the
Epstein-Barr virus causes a frequently fatal child-
hood cancer called Burkitt lymphoma as well as the
nonmalignant disease infectious mononucleosis.
The herpesvirus cytomegalovirus lies dormant in the
tissues of most humans and can be induced to cause
fatal diseases in infants and immunocompromised

adults. A different herpesvirus causes chickenpox (varicella); the same virus lies latent in the tissues for long periods of time (perhaps years or decades) and later undergoes recrudescence (the recurrence of symptoms after they have abated) to cause the painful skin and neurological disease called herpes zoster, or shingles. In addition, there are herpesviruses that cause disease in animals—for example, the widespread and usually fatal disease in chickens called Marek's disease. The widespread distribution of viruses of the family Herpesviridae is evident from other diseases in monkeys and frogs.

The viruses of the family Retroviridae are perhaps the most widely distributed of the transforming viruses that infect eukaryotic cells ranging from yeast to humans. It was suggested early in the 20th century that viruses cause leukemias and lymphomas in birds. In 1911 the American pathologist Peyton Rous first described a virus that causes sarcomas in chickens.

The virions of retroviruses are spherical (or polygonal) and are surrounded by a lipid membrane containing a glycoprotein that recognizes and binds to cell receptors of a particular species (type-specific glycoproteins). Retrovirus genomes consist of two identical RNA molecules, each with 7,000 to 10,000 nucleotides. Associated with the virion RNA is an enzyme, an RNA-dependent DNA polymerase, also called a reverse transcriptase.

Using the virion RNA as a template, the reverse transcriptase catalyzes the synthesis of a linear DNA molecule complementary to the virion RNA. The new complementary strand of DNA also serves as a template for the reverse transcriptase, which makes a second anticomplementary DNA molecule, thus forming double-stranded DNA. The genomic RNA of fully infectious bird retroviruses, those that can replicate autonomously, has four genes that code sequentially for group-specific antigens, the reverse transcriptase, the envelope glycoprotein, and the sarcoma-transforming protein. At each end of the genome are homologous flanking nucleotide sequences, known as long terminal repeats (LTR), which code for double-stranded DNA that can recognize host cell DNA sequences for integration of the proviral DNA into the host cell chromosome. Many retroviruses are defective and cannot replicate in cells without helper (nondefective) retroviruses. The helper retroviruses generally transform fibroblastic cells, resulting in malignant sarcomas, whereas the defective retroviruses transform blood-cell precursors, resulting in leukemias.

Many different retroviruses have been identified as causative agents of cancers in birds, rodents (particularly mice), domestic cats, monkeys, and humans. Certain lymphatic leukemias in humans are caused by human T-cell leukemia virus (HTLV); acquired immune deficiency syndrome (AIDS) is

REVERSE TRANSCRIPTASE

Reverse transcriptase, also called RNA-directed DNA polymerase, is an enzyme encoded from the genetic material of retroviruses that catalyzes the transcription of retrovirus RNA (ribonucleic acid) into DNA (deoxyribonucleic acid). This catalyzed transcription is the reverse process of normal cellular transcription of DNA into RNA, hence the names *reverse transcriptase* and *retrovirus*. Reverse transcriptase is central to the infectious nature of retroviruses, several of which cause disease in humans, including human immunodeficiency virus (HIV), which causes acquired immunodeficiency syndrome (AIDS), and human T-cell lymphotrophic virus I (HTLV-I), which causes leukemia. Reverse transcriptase is also a fundamental component of a laboratory technology known as reverse transcription-polymerase chain reaction (RT-PCR), a powerful tool used in research and in the diagnosis of diseases such as cancer.

Retroviruses consist of an RNA genome contained within a protein shell that is enclosed in a lipid envelope. The retrovirus genome is typically made up of three genes: the group-specific antigen gene (gag), the polymerase gene (pol), and the envelope gene (env). The pol gene encodes the three enzymes—protease, reverse transcriptase, and integrase—that catalyze the steps of retroviral infection. Once a retrovirus is inside a host cell (a process mediated by protease), it takes over the host's genetic transcription machinery

(c(Continued on page 190)

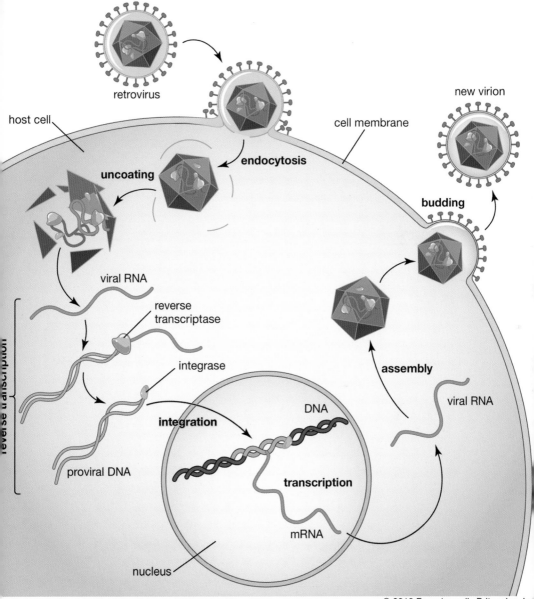

Following retrovirus infection, reverse transcriptase converts viral RNA into proviral DNA, which is then incorporated into the DNA of the host cell in the nucleus.

(continued from page 188)

to construct a DNA provirus. This process, the conversion of retroviral RNA to proviral DNA, is catalyzed by reverse transcriptase and is necessary for proviral DNA insertion into host DNA—a step initiated by the integrase enzyme.

For many years there existed a paradigm in molecular biology known as the "central dogma." This asserted that DNA is first transcribed into RNA, RNA is translated into amino acids, and amino acids assemble into long chains, called polypeptides, that make up proteins—the functional units of cellular life. However, while this central dogma is true, as with many paradigms of biology, important exceptions can be found.

The first important observations opposing the central dogma came in the early 20th century. In 1911 American pathologist Peyton Rous, working at the Rockefeller Institute for Medical Research (now Rockefeller University), reported that healthy chickens developed malignant sarcomas (cancers of connective tissues) when infected with tumour cells from other chickens. Rous investigated the tumour cells further, and from them, he isolated a virus, which was later named Rous sarcoma virus (RSV). Decades later the significance of his discoveries was realized, and in 1966—more than 55 years after his first experiment, at the age of 87— Rous was awarded the Nobel Prize for Physiology or Medicine for his discovery of tumour-inducing viruses.

By the 1960s it was understood that sarcomas are caused by a mutation that results in uncontrolled cell division. It was also evident that RSV was inherited during the division of cancerous cells. Scientists hypothesized that, in order for such viral inheritance to occur, a virus would need to transcribe its RNA genome into DNA and then insert this DNA into the host cell genome. Once incorporated into the host genome, the virus would be transcribed as though it were another gene and could produce more RNA virus from its DNA. This hypothesis, called the "DNA provirus hypothesis," was developed in the late 1950s by American virologist Howard Martin Temin, when he was a postdoctoral fellow in the laboratory of Italian virologist Renato Dulbecco at the California Institute of Technology. Temin's hypothesis was formally proposed in 1964. The provirus hypothesis came about when experiments demonstrated that an antibiotic called actinomycin D, which is capable of inhibiting DNA and RNA synthesis, inhibited the reproduction of RSV. In 1970 Temin and Japanese virologist Satoshi Mizutani, and American virologist David Baltimore, working independently, reported the discovery of an enzyme that could synthesize proviral DNA from the RNA genome of RSV. This enzyme was named RNA-directed DNA polymerase, commonly referred to as reverse transcriptase. This discovery resulted in the identification of a unique virus family (Retroviridae), and the understanding of the pathogenesis of these viruses spurred a rush to discover other infectious cancer-causing agents.

(continued on the next page)

(continued from the previous page)

In the early 1980s the HTLV-I and HTLV-II retroviruses were discovered and found to cause leukemia. In 1983 HIV was isolated and identified as the causative agent of AIDS. HIV infects white blood cells known as helper T cells and results in the production of more virus and, eventually, cell death and destruction of the immune system. Drugs that inhibit reverse transcriptase were the first treatments available to people living with HIV. Nucleoside reverse transcriptase inhibitors (NRTIs) such as AZT (zidovudine)—the first drug approved by the U.S. Food and Drug Administration to prolong the lives of AIDS patients—act by terminating the proviral DNA chain before the enzyme can finish transcription. NRTIs are often given in combination with non-nucleoside reverse transcriptase inhibitors (NNRTIs) such as efavirenz that act by binding to and altering the shape of the enzyme itself, thereby blocking the enzyme's function.

The ability of reverse transcriptase to synthesize DNA from RNA has been used in the laboratory. For example, RT-PCR is commonly used to quantify the amount of messenger RNA (mRNA) transcribed from a gene. Because RNA is fragile and difficult to study, a strand of complementary DNA (cDNA) is synthesized from RNA, using reverse transcriptase during the RT-PCR procedure. The cDNA can then be amplified by polymerase chain reaction and used for subsequent experiments.

caused by a retrovirus called human immunodeficiency virus (HIV).

Retroviruses originated from genes in many different species of animals and even lower forms of life. Individual retroviruses are limited in their host range and do not readily cross species barriers. Virtually every retrovirus studied to date is analogous to the genes normally found in animals (including humans), known as proto-oncogenes, genes that are involved with regulating normal cell growth and development and which also have the potential to change into cancer-causing genes. These proto-oncogenes have deoxynucleotide sequences closely, but not entirely, homologous (i.e., of the same type and order) to the nucleotide sequences of a corresponding viral cancer-causing gene, called an oncogene. Integration of retrovirus DNA into cell chromosomes results in cancer, but the proto-oncogenes do not become cancer-causing genes unless triggered by another event.

ROLE OF VIRUSES IN DISEASE

Although viruses were originally discovered and characterized on the basis of the diseases they cause, most viruses that infect bacteria, plants, and animals (including humans) do not cause disease. In fact, bacteriophages may be helpful in that they rapidly transfer genetic information from one bacterium to another, and viruses of plants and animals may convey genetic information among similar species, helping their hosts survive in hostile environments. In the future this could also be true for humans. Recombinant DNA biotechnology shows great promise for the repair of genetic defects. Afflicted persons are injected with cells transformed by viruses that carry a functional copy of the defective human gene. The virus integrates the normal gene into the DNA of the human cell.

Of those viruses that cause disease, some cause short-term (acute) diseases and others recurring or long-term (chronic) diseases. Some viruses cause acute disease from which there is fairly rapid recovery but may persist in the tissues, remaining dormant for long periods of time, and then become active again, bringing about serious disease decades later. Slowly progressive viruses have long incubation periods before the onset of disease. As mentioned above, the DNA of certain viruses becomes integrated into the genome of the host cell, often resulting in malignant transformation of cells, which become cancers.

The nature of the disease caused by a virus is generally a genetic property of the virus as well as of the host cells. Many viruses, however, can remain dormant in the tissues of the host (latency). Viruses that cause acute disease are generally, but not always, those that rapidly harm or destroy cells (cytopathic effects) and have the capacity to shut off protein or nucleic acid synthesis within the host cell.

Human poliovirus and related picornaviruses that infect other animal species are examples of acute infectious agents that shut down protein synthesis in the host cell soon after infection; these picornaviruses also inhibit cellular RNA and DNA synthesis. Another virus that rapidly kills the infected cell is the negative-strand vesicular stomatitis virus (VSV) of the family Rhabdoviridae; viral RNA newly synthesized by infectious VSV rapidly shuts off cellular RNA synthesis and, to a somewhat lesser extent, cellular protein synthesis. In both poliovirus and VSV, the infected cell dies within hours of the inhibition of cellular RNA and protein synthesis. Influenza A viruses of the family Orthomyxoviridae, which cause a highly contagious respiratory disease in humans, inhibit cellular macromolecular synthesis by several unique mechanisms, including blocking the maturation of cellular mRNAs and cleaving off the ends of cellular mRNAs in the nucleus of infected cells. Other viruses that inhibit cellular macromolecule synthesis and produce acute infections include the poxviruses, reoviruses, togaviruses, adenoviruses, and herpesviruses; the latter two persist in host tissues for long periods of time and cause chronic infection as well.

Many, if not most, diseases resulting from viral infection of vertebrates are caused not by a direct effect of the virus but rather by a secondary immune response. Essentially all viral proteins are recognized by vertebrate animals as immunologically foreign, and the immune systems of these animals mount two kinds of immune response, humoral and cellular. In humoral immunity, B lymphocytes, usually triggered by helper T lymphocytes, make antibodies (proteins that recognize and bind foreign molecules) to the viral protein. The antibody synthesized as a result of the immune response against a specific viral antigen usually benefits the infected host because that antibody can neutralize the infectivity of the specific virus in the blood and tissues of the infected host. Viruses inside the cell are not accessible to the antibody, because it cannot cross the cell membrane barrier.

In cellular immunity, a killer T cell recognizes and kills a virus-infected cell because of the viral antigen on its surface, thus aborting the infection because a virus will not grow within a dead cell. If the virus-infected cells are not essential for host functions, the killer T cell can prevent the spread of the infecting virus to other cells and distant tissues. Not infrequently, the virus-specific T lymphocyte kills vital cells such as nerve cells (neurons), muscle cells, and liver cells, all of which carry out important functions. In addition, the death of cells results in an inflammatory response, which also can damage vital tissues. Therefore, the cellular immune response to a viral infection can cause disease. In general, diseases caused by chronic viral infections, but also occasionally by subacute (between acute and chronic) viral infections, are caused by cellular immune responses that damage the virus-infected tissue.

INFECTIOUS PATTERNS

Acute viral infections are of two types—local and systemic—both usually resulting from a direct effect of the invading virus on host tissue cells. Acute local infections generally occur at the site of viral infection. For example, acute respiratory infections include (1) the common cold, in which the rhinovirus infects only the nasal mucosa, (2) influenza, in which the virus is found in both nasal and bronchial mucosa, where severe damage can result in death, (3) flu-like illnesses caused by adenoviruses localized in lymphoid tissue of the throat (although infection also can occur in the intestine and the eye or be spread to the heart), and (4) severe respiratory infections of infants and children, caused by parainfluenza viruses or respiratory syncytial viruses, which may be life-threatening. Examples of acute infections localized to the intestine include those that result in enteritis (bowel inflammation), which may be accompanied by diarrhea; these are often caused by rotaviruses and coronaviruses.

Many viruses transmitted by the respiratory route (from sneezes and coughs, for example) and limited to humans begin their cycle of infection in the upper respiratory tract (nose and throat) and then enter the bloodstream, where they are spread to distant tissues. Examples of such diseases are measles, mumps, and chickenpox, in which the growth of the specific virus in the mucosal cells of the throat during the first few days of infection usually results in mild fever and achiness; this stage is called the prodromal period of the illness. During the next few days, the virus enters the draining lymph nodes and then the bloodstream, where it is spread throughout the tissues of the body, resulting in fever and rash (in the case of measles and chickenpox) and inflammation of the parotid glands and, less frequently, the testes, ovaries, and joints (in the case of mumps). Varicella (chickenpox) virus rarely causes pneumonia, but all these viruses can cause meningitis and, rarely, encephalitis. A similar pattern of infection formerly occurred with smallpox, a disease that was more frequently fatal but now ostensibly has been eradicated.

A large number of viruses of the digestive tract (enteroviruses)—among them poliovirus, Coxsackie viruses, and echoviruses (enteric cytopathic human orphan virus)—also cause a two-phase illness. Enteroviruses grow initially in the intestinal tract and are transmitted by mouth through water, food, and other materials contaminated with feces. The viruses are resistant to the acid normally found in the stomach and thus reach the intestinal tract, where they multiply in living mucosal cells. This initial period of viral invasion and growth in the intestine causes either an initial mild febrile illness or is asymptomatic. Over the next few days these enteroviruses are spread from the intestinal mucosa to the draining lymph nodes, from which they invade the bloodstream, resulting in a condition known as viremia. From the bloodstream the viruses are widely spread to all tissues, but in most cases no symptomatic disease occurs. Poliovirus in less than 1 percent of cases affects the spinal cord or brain, resulting in paralysis or death. Different types of Coxsackie viruses and echoviruses can cause acute, usually nonfatal, illnesses such as meningitis, carditis, pleurisy, or rashes.

Many viral diseases are transmitted by bites of insects or other arthropods, and these infections usually begin in the skin or lymph nodes and rapidly invade the bloodstream. The nature of the disease caused by these arthropod-borne viruses (arboviruses) is determined by the affinity (tropism) of each virus for specific organs. Many that have an affinity for brain tissue cause encephalitis or meningitis, but others primarily infect the muscles, liver, heart, or kidneys. Virtually all these diseases are epidemic in character, and the viruses that cause them are the primary pathogens of birds and mammals. The insect, usually a certain species of mosquito, takes a blood meal from the infected host bird or mammal and shortly thereafter bites a human, thus transmitting the virus. These arboviruses do not ordinarily multiply in the insect but simply reside on its proboscis. Examples of human epidemic diseases resulting from transmission of these often fatal arboviruses are encephalitis caused by viruses of the families Togaviridae and Flaviviridae, yellow fever and dengue caused by viruses of the family Flaviviridae, and hemorrhagic fevers caused by viruses of the families Bunyaviridae and Arenaviridae. Of considerable interest and concern is the identification of new strains of viruses, particularly a hantavirus of the Bunyaviridae family that was responsible for an epidemic in the early 1990s in the southwestern United States that resulted in considerable numbers of fatal human infections.

LATENCY

Inapparent infections (those that do not cause specific signs and symptoms) often result after exposure to picornaviruses, influenza viruses, rhinoviruses, herpesviruses, and adenoviruses but less frequently to measles and chickenpox viruses. In cases of inapparent infection, long-lasting immunity develops, but only to the strain of virus that has the same antigenic composition as the original infecting virus.

Certain of these viruses persist in the tissues of the host after the initial infection despite the presence of circulating antibodies to it in the blood and tissues. Such viruses probably reside inside cells, where they are protected from antibodies that cannot penetrate the cell membrane. Among persistent viruses are adenoviruses, measles virus, and, in particular, many kinds of herpesviruses. The genetic information of herpesviruses and adenoviruses can be integrated into the genome of the host cell, but it is believed that these viruses frequently, and the measles virus invariably, reside in cells in the form of extrachromosomal genes (genes not integrated in chromosomes). These dormant viruses can be activated by many factors, such as trauma, another

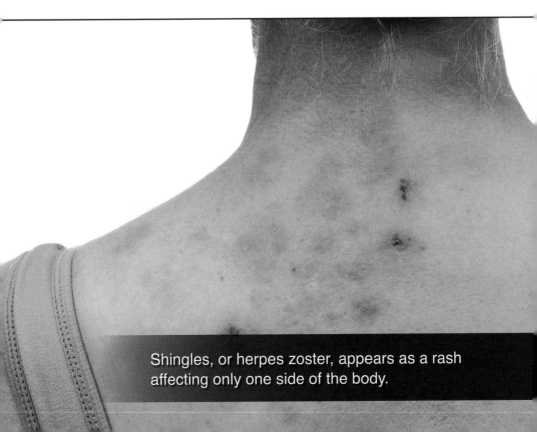

Shingles, or herpes zoster, appears as a rash affecting only one side of the body.

infection, emotional stress, menstruation, excessive exposure to sunlight, and various illnesses.

The phenomenon of latency and reactivation is particularly common among viruses of the family Herpesviridae, which cause chronic or recurrent diseases: (1) herpes simplex virus type 1, which causes recurrent cold sores, (2) herpes simplex virus type 2 in genital tissue, which causes repeated herpetic infections of the vagina or penis, (3) cytomegalovirus, which usually produces an inapparent infection activated by simultaneously occurring disease to cause severe liver, lung, or nervous-system disease, and (4) varicella virus, which is the causative agent of chickenpox but which can be activated decades later to produce herpes zoster (shingles). A rare, but invariably fatal, disease of the nervous system is subacute sclerosing panencephalitis (SSPE), which is a progressive, degenerative condition caused by measles virus (a paramyxovirus) lying dormant in brain cells for many years and then reactivated, usually in adolescence. There is no simple explanation for why latent viruses, such as those in the family Herpesviridae, that are present in the tissues of most adult humans can be activated to cause disease in some people but not in others.

CHRONIC AND SLOWLY PROGRESSIVE DISEASES

Although some viruses multiply slowly, this is not always the explanation for the chronicity or the slow progression of the diseases caused by these viruses. Hepatitis, for example, is a subacute or chronic disease, with a long latent period, that is caused by at least five viruses with different properties. Hepatitis A is caused by a picornavirus usually transmitted by the fecal-oral route in a manner similar to that of poliovirus. Hepatitis B is caused by a small DNA virus that contains its own DNA polymerase and is transmitted by transfusion of blood and other blood products, by the sharing of nonsterile hypodermic needles among drug users, by sexual intercourse, or from mother to neonate. Hepatitis B virus is classified with similar viruses of birds in the family Hepadnaviridae. Most cases of hepatitis spread by the transfusion of blood or blood products or by needles shared by drug users are caused by a third, completely distinct virus—originally called non-A, non-B hepatitis but now known to be a member of the virus family Flaviviridae—designated hepatitis C virus. A fourth unique agent that causes hepatitis is designated hepatitis delta virus, which has not yet been classified taxonomically but is a small, enveloped virus containing a circular RNA genome; hepatitis B virus serves as a helper for replication of hepatitis delta virus, the virions of which contain hepatitis B surface antigen (HB_sAg). The fifth causative agent of viral hepatitis, largely occurring in Asia and Africa, is a small RNA virus tentatively classified as a member of the family Caliciviridae and designated hepatitis E virus.

Many other agents that appear to cause chronic and slowly progressive diseases, particularly those affecting the nervous system, have been identified. A fatal neurological disorder of sheep, called scrapie, has an incubation period of years and may be caused by a heat-resistant protein called a prion, which is self-replicating. Similar, rather obscure agents have been identified for two uncommon fatal disorders of the nervous system called Creutzfeldt-Jakob disease and kuru.

The disease now known as AIDS was first recognized in homosexuals and hemophiliacs about 1981 and continues to be disseminated throughout the world. Today it is one of the most devastating pandemics of all time. AIDS is caused by HIV, a member of a genetically more complex group of the family Retroviridae called lentiviruses. Closely related viruses of monkeys and cats cause similar diseases. HIV is transmitted by blood and other body fluids and infects primarily helper T lymphocytes and other cells with CD4 surface receptors (cell surface proteins that react with antigens), to which the virus binds. After the virus has been dormant for years, destruction of T lymphocytes results in drastic depression of the immune system. Death almost invariably results from "opportunistic" infections such as pneumonia—caused by ordinarily nonpathogenic organisms such as *Pneumocystis carinii*—or tuberculosis or by cancers such as Kaposi sarcoma and lymphomas.

CONTROLLING VIRAL INFECTION

Unlike bacteria, viruses mimic the metabolic functions of their host cells. Antibiotics are not effective against viruses. It is difficult to identify chemical compounds that inhibit the multiplication of viruses but do not slow the functions of, or are not toxic to, the host cell. The spread of many viral diseases can be prevented by hygienic factors such as efficient sanitation facilities, effective waste disposal, clean water, and personal cleanliness.

VACCINES

Active immunization by vaccines (antigen-containing preparations that elicit the synthesis of antibodies and thus immunity) has been useful in preventing common epidemics caused by acutely infectious viruses.

The best example of such a preventable disease is smallpox, caused by a disease-producing virus that at one time was found worldwide. In 1796 English physician Edward Jenner discovered that the milder cowpox virus could serve as a live vaccine (an antigenic preparation consisting of viruses whose disease-producing capacity has been weakened) for preventing smallpox. Jenner published his findings in 1798. The program of vaccination that resulted from Jenner's discovery is one of the greatest success stories in the annals of medicine. In 1980 the World

In the 19th century, English doctors used small blades, such as those seen above, to cut a patient's skin and administer the smallpox vaccine.

Health Organization declared that the disease had been eliminated.

A different prospect is presented by rabies, an invariably fatal viral disease mentioned in ancient Greek literature. Transmitted by the bite of dogs and other domestic and wild animals, the rabies virus is more difficult to eradicate because it is present in wild animals throughout the world, except in certain island countries such as Great Britain and Australia. Influenza virus is also distributed worldwide, but, of the three major immunologic types, only one (type A) is responsible for epidemics and pandemics.

The worldwide pandemic of influenza at the end of World War I is estimated to have caused between 25 million and 50 million deaths, mostly of adolescents and young adults. Because of virus mutations that produce minor antigenic changes every year and major antigenic shifts about every 10 years, influenza viruses have the capacity to resist inactivation by antibodies acquired by previous infection or vaccination. Development of effective vaccines to combat influenza is a difficult task, although existing vaccines are partially effective and are recommended for people at high risk—i.e., the elderly and those with chronic disease of the respiratory or circulatory systems.

Vaccines are most successful when directed against those viruses that do not mutate and that infect only humans. In addition to smallpox, a successful vaccine program has been carried out against polio. Polioviruses exist in only three antigenic types, each of which has not changed significantly for decades. The vaccines available are the "killed" (Salk) vaccine, composed of inactivated virus of the three types, and the "live" (Sabin) vaccine, composed of genetically attenuated viruses of the three types. These vaccines, which were introduced in the 1950s and '60s, respectively, have lowered the incidence in developed countries of paralysis resulting from polio. The disease still occurs in developing countries and recurs in some developed countries where vaccination programs have not been enforced. Rare cases of polio occur from the Sabin vaccine strain of type-3 poliovirus, which is genetically unstable and occasionally reverts to the virulent form.

Vaccination can prevent diseases caused by strictly human viruses that exist in only one antigenic and stable type. Measles has been prevented in developed countries with routine vaccination. Measles, however, may still be the major cause of death in children in developing countries. Vaccination for mumps and chickenpox promises to be successful because the causative viruses of these diseases show little tendency to vary antigenically and are confined to humans. On the other hand, development of vaccines for the common cold caused by rhinoviruses, similar to polioviruses, will be a formidable, if not impossible, task because there are at least 100 antigenic types of the rhinovirus. Also daunting is the task of developing a vaccine against HIV. The major antigenic component of this virus is a surface-membrane-inserted glycoprotein (gp120), which has a startling rate of mutation. The extreme antigenic diversity that results from the mutability of the gene that codes for this protein would prevent HIV from being identified and attacked by circulating antibodies or killer T lymphocytes.

ANTIVIRAL DRUGS

An effective antiviral drug has been developed against influenza virus. This drug targets a viral enzyme called the neuraminidase and is orders of magnitude less active against nonviral neuraminidases. These neuraminidase inhibitors are most effective when administered prophylactically or within the first 30 hours of symptom onset and can be used to limit the spread of influenza virus and to complement the administration of vaccines. Other chemicals that exert a selectively greater effect on viral replication than they do on cell replication include ribavirin, acyclovir, and zidovudine (azidothymidine [AZT]). These

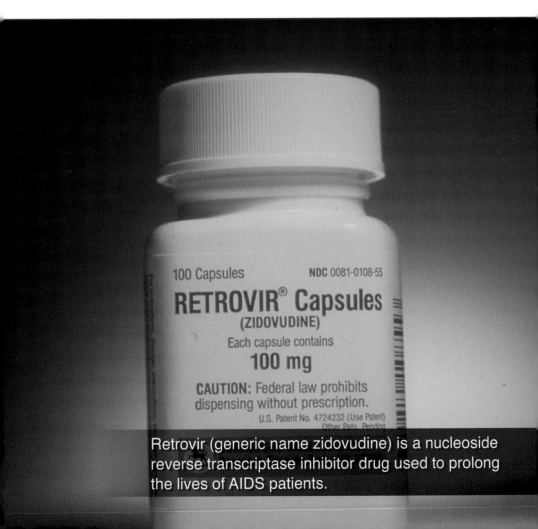

Retrovir (generic name zidovudine) is a nucleoside reverse transcriptase inhibitor drug used to prolong the lives of AIDS patients.

drugs have been partially effective in improving, if not curing, viral diseases without causing major toxic side effects. AZT has been used with some success in prolonging the lives of patients with AIDS.

Certain natural products of cells, called interferons, may have potential antiviral and anticancer properties. Interferons are proteins normally synthesized by the cells of vertebrates, including humans, either intrinsically and without stimulation or in response to certain viral infections, chemicals, or immune reactions. In general, the multiplication of viruses is inhibited by interferons, some to a much greater extent than others. Interferons are generally species-specific; i.e., they are effective in inhibiting viral infection only in cells of the same species that naturally synthesize the interferon.

There are three classes of interferons: α-interferons, produced by blood leukocytes; β-interferons, produced by tissue cells and fibroblasts; and γ-interferons (also called immune interferons or interleukins), produced by immune reactions in blood lymphocytes. Interferons are now known to be a subset of a large group of natural cellular substances called cytokines, which signal cells to perform specific functions. Until recently, interferons were difficult to produce commercially because cells and tissues synthesize only small amounts of them. Through recombinant DNA technology, however, large amounts of interferon can be produced.

There has been some success in using interferons to treat viral diseases, such as colds caused by rhinoviruses, infections caused by herpesviruses, and benign tumours and warts caused by papillomaviruses. Local administration at the sites of viral infection affords the best results, although injections of large amounts of interferons can be harmful, probably because they tend to inhibit protein synthesis in the host cell.

TYPES OF VIRUSES

There are many different types of viruses, which are divided into genera and species that are assigned to higher groups, such as families and orders. Viruses are classified on the basis of their nucleic acid content, their size, the shape of their protein capsid, and the presence of a surrounding lipoprotein envelope. The nucleic acid content and its organization, such as whether it occurs in single or double strands, forms the basis for the division of viruses at the higher taxonomic levels.

CLASSIFICATION FEATURES

The primary taxonomic division of viruses is into two classes based on nucleic acid content: DNA viruses or RNA viruses. The DNA viruses are subdivided into those that contain either double-stranded or single-stranded DNA. The RNA viruses also are divided into those that contain double-stranded or single-stranded RNA. Further subdivision of the RNA viruses is based on whether the RNA genome is segmented or not. If the viruses contain single-stranded RNA as their genetic information, they are divided into positive-strand viruses if the RNA is of messenger sense (directly translatable into proteins) or negative-strand viruses if the RNA must be transcribed by a polymerase into mRNA.

All viruses falling into one of these nucleic acid classifications are further subdivided on the basis of whether the nucleocapsid (protein coat and enclosed nucleic acid) assumes a rodlike or a polygonal (usually icosahedral) shape. The icosahedral viruses are further subdivided into families based on the number of capsomeres making up the capsids. Finally, all viruses fall into two classes depending on whether the nucleocapsid is surrounded by a lipoprotein envelope.

Some virologists adhere to a division of viruses into those that infect bacteria, plants, or animals; these classifications have some validity, particularly for the unique bacterial viruses with tails, but there is otherwise so much overlap that taxonomy based on hosts seems unworkable. Classification based on diseases caused by viruses also is not tenable, because closely related viruses frequently do not cause the same disease. Eventually, it is likely that the classification of viruses will be based on their nucleotide sequences and their mode of replication, rather than on structural components, as is now the case.

The basic taxonomic group is called a family, designated by the suffix -*viridae*. The major taxonomic disagreement among virologists is whether to segregate viruses within a family into a specific genus and further subdivide them into species names. In the first decade of the 21st century, there occurred a shift toward the use of binomial nomenclature— as used for bacteria—dividing viruses into italicized genera and species. This move was prompted in large part by the International Committee on Taxonomy of Viruses (ICTV), a member group of the International Union of Microbiological Societies. The ICTV oversees the ongoing process of devising and maintaining a universal classification scheme for viruses. In the virus classification hierarchy, the ICTV recognizes orders, families, subfamilies, genera, and species. The placement of viruses in these groups is based on information provided by study groups comprised of experts on specific types of viruses.

In the ICTV system, each species of virus is generally recognized as representing a group of isolates, or viruses with distinct nucleic acid sequences. Thus, a single species of virus may sometimes contain more than one isolate. Although the isolates of a species possess unique genetic sequences, they all descend from the same replicating lineage and therefore share particular genetic traits. Furthermore, isolates of a species also share in common the ability to thrive within a specific ecological niche. As scientists identify new isolates and species, the classification of viruses is expected to become increasingly complex. The following sections present examples of well characterized DNA and RNA viruses as they are classified based on the ICTV system.

MAJOR GROUPS OF DNA VIRUSES

DNA viruses contain either double-stranded or single-stranded DNA, and as a group they are characterized by a diverse array of mechanisms of infection and replication within host cells. DNA viruses can cause various diseases in plants and animals, with herpesviruses and parvoviruses serving as examples of important animal pathogens.

ADENOVIRUS

An adenovirus is any virus belonging to the family Adenoviridae. This group of viruses was discovered in the 1950s and includes about 50 species (formerly referred to as serotypes) that cause sore throat and fever in humans, hepatitis in dogs, and several diseases in fowl, mice, cattle, pigs, and monkeys. The virus particle lacks an outer envelope and is spheroidal, about 80 nm (1 nm = 10^{-9} metre) across. It is covered with 252 regularly arranged capsid protein

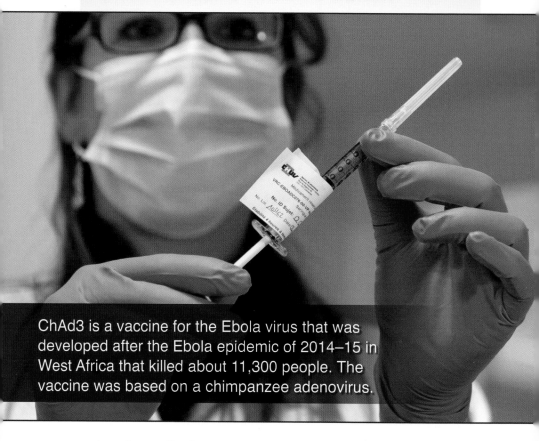

ChAd3 is a vaccine for the Ebola virus that was developed after the Ebola epidemic of 2014–15 in West Africa that killed about 11,300 people. The vaccine was based on a chimpanzee adenovirus.

subunits called capsomeres and has a core of double-stranded DNA wrapped in a protective coat of protein. Adenoviruses develop within the nuclei of infected cells, where they are often observed packed in an apparently crystalline arrangement.

In humans, adenoviruses cause acute mucous membrane infections of the upper respiratory tract, the eyes, and frequently the regional lymph nodes, bearing considerable resemblance to the common cold. Adenoviruses can also cause epidemic keratoconjunctivitis (EKC) and are considered to be responsible for an outbreak of respiratory disease among military recruits in 1997. Like the cold viruses, adenoviruses are often found in latent infections in clinically healthy persons. Of the many different adenovirus species, only a few commonly cause illness in humans. Thus, it is possible to prepare a vaccine against these viruses. Vaccines include a first-generation inactivated vaccine against several adenovirus types and a non-attenuated oral vaccine against adenovirus types 4 and 7. In contrast, there are more than 100 cold viruses, all of which are commonly found as disease agents. This great number makes the development of a vaccine for the common cold virtually impossible.

ASFARVIRUS

An asfarvirus is any virus belonging to the family Asfarviridae. This family consists of one genus, *Asfivirus*, which contains the African swine fever virus. Asfarviruses have enveloped virions that are approximately 175–215 nm in diameter. An icosahedral capsid (the protein shell surrounding the viral nucleic acids) contains linear double-stranded DNA.

The African swine fever virus is believed to circulate between soft-bodied ticks (*Ornithodoros*) and pigs, specifically wild pigs (*Sus scrofa*), warthogs (*Phacochoerus aethiopicus*), and bush pigs (*Potamochoerus porcus*). The virus is found primarily in sub-Saharan Africa.

HEPADNAVIRUS

Hepadnaviruses are infectious agents belonging to the family Hepadnaviridae. Hepadnaviruses have small, enveloped, spherical virions that are about 40–48 nm in diameter. The capsid contains a circular double-stranded DNA molecule with a single-stranded DNA region and a DNA-dependent DNA polymerase. The polymerase enzyme functions to repair the gap in the double-stranded DNA molecule that is created by the presence of the segment of single-stranded DNA. The activity of the polymerase is essential for the virus's replication. Hepadnaviruses are further distinguished by the use of reverse transcriptase for replication and by an abundance of the soluble protein HB_sAg (hepatitis B surface antigen).

There are two recognized genera of hepadnavirus: *Orthohepadnavirus* and *Avihepadnavirus*. The former includes hepatitis B viruses that have been isolated from mammals, including humans, woodchucks, ground squirrels, Arctic squirrels, and woolly monkeys. The second genus, *Avihepadnavirus*, consists of hepatitis B viruses that infect birds, including ducks, herons, cranes, and storks. There are also several other hepadnaviruses that infect Ross geese and snow geese, though these are less well characterized.

Humans and other animals that become infected with hepatitis B virus may develop a severe and long-lasting form of liver disease known as hepati-

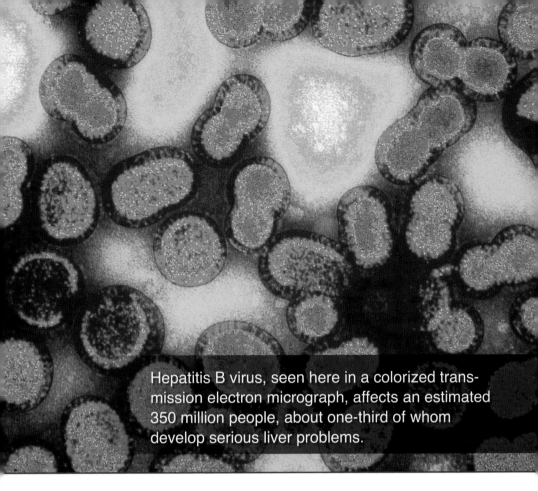

Hepatitis B virus, seen here in a colorized transmission electron micrograph, affects an estimated 350 million people, about one-third of whom develop serious liver problems.

tis. In humans the condition may occur as an acute disease, or in about 5 to 10 percent of cases it may become chronic and lead to permanent liver damage. Symptoms usually appear from 40 days to 6 months after exposure to the virus. Those persons at greatest risk for contracting hepatitis B include intravenous drug users, sexual partners of individuals with the disease, health care workers who are not adequately immunized, and recipients of organ transplants or blood transfusions. A safe and effective vaccine against the virus is available and provides protection for at least five years. Passive immunization with hepatitis B immune globulin (antibody) can also provide protection. Approximately 1 in 10 patients infected with hepatitis B virus becomes a virus carrier and may transmit it to others. Those who carry hepatitis B virus are also 100 times more likely to develop liver cancer than persons who do not carry the virus in their blood.

HERPESVIRUS

A herpesvirus is any virus belonging to the family Herpesviridae. These viruses are pathogenic in a wide variety of animals, causing disease in humans, monkeys, birds, frogs, and fish. The herpesviruses are characterized structurally by virions measuring approximately 150–200 nm in diameter. The outer surface of the capsid is icosahedral and is composed of 162 capsomeres. The capsid itself is surrounded by a lipid envelope containing glycoprotein spikes. Herpesviruses have genomes consisting of linear double-stranded DNA, which is integrated into the host cell chromosome upon infection.

There are three known subfamilies of herpesviruses: Alphaherpesvirinae, Betaherpesvirinae, and Gammaherpesvirinae. Alphaherpesvirinae contains the human herpes simplex viruses types 1 and 2, which are grouped in the genus Simplexvirus, along with bovine mamillitis virus and spider monkey herpesvirus. Other genera in the subfamily include Varicellovirus, which contains pseudorabies virus, equine herpesvirus, and varicella-zoster virus (the causative agent of chickenpox); Mardivirus, which contains Marek's disease viruses types 1 and 2 of chickens and turkey herpesvirus; and Iltovirus, which contains gallid herpesvirus 1. The alphaherpesviruses are distinguished from viruses of the other subfamilies by their fast rate of replication.

Betaherpesvirinae, members of which are noted for their relatively slow replication cycles, contains human, rhesus monkey, African green monkey, and chimpanzee cytomegaloviruses (genus *Cytomegalovirus*). Members of subfamily Gammaherpesvirinae, which is composed of the genera *Lymphocryptovirus*, *Macavirus*, *Percavirus*, and *Rhadinovirus*, include Epstein-Barr virus, baboon, orangutan, and gorilla herpesviruses, and herpesvirus saimiri. The replication rate of gammaherpesviruses is variable.

Among the best-characterized herpesviruses are those affecting humans, namely herpes simplex virus type 1 (HSV-1) and herpes simplex virus type 2 (HSV-2). Whereas HSV-1 is transmitted orally and is responsible for cold sores and fever blisters, typically occurring around the mouth, HSV-2 is transmitted sexually and is the main cause of the condition known as genital herpes. HSV-1 may also infect the eye, causing corneal ulcers and visual impairment. Both viruses are highly contagious. HSV-2 may be transmitted by individuals who are lifelong carriers but who remain asymptomatic (and may not even know they are infected). HSV-2 infections have also been associated with the development of cervical cancer.

IRIDOVIRUS

An iridovirus is any virus belonging to the family Iridoviridae. Iridoviruses possess large enveloped or non-enveloped virions that measure 120–350 nm in diameter. The capsid is icosahedral and contains linear double-stranded DNA. Among the genera included in this family are *Iridovirus*, *Chloriridovirus*, *Lymphocystivirus*, *Ranavirus*, and *Megalocytivirus*. Type species of the family include invertebrate iridescent virus 6 (*Iridovirus*), which infects insects; lymphocystis disease virus 1 (*Lymphocystivirus*), which infects fish; and frog virus 3 (*Ranavirus*), which infects amphibians.

PAPILLOMAVIRUS

Papillomaviruses are infectious agents belonging to the family Papillomaviridae. These viruses are known for causing infections in birds and mammals that result in warts (papillomas) and other benign tumours. In humans they can cause malignant cancers of the genital tract and the uterine cervix.

They are small polygonal viruses containing circular double-stranded DNA. More than 100 distinct types of human papillomaviruses (HPVs) have been identified by DNA analysis, and there are numerous types of animal papillomaviruses, including bovine papillomavirus (BPV), canine oral papillomavirus (COPV), and cottontail rabbit papillomavirus (CRPV; or Shope papillomavirus).

Skin warts are the most common sign of infection with papillomavirus. In humans warts may be of two types—flat (which are superficial and usually on the hands) or plantar (on the soles of the feet and on the toes). Warts also commonly occur on the genitals (condylomata acuminata). In humans and most other animals, papillomas—whether found on the skin or occurring in the mucous membranes of the genital, anal, or oral cavities—are benign and may actually go unnoticed for years. In humans a minority of genital and venereal warts are visible, painful, or itchy, and the papillomaviruses that cause these warts are transmitted by sexual intercourse. It is estimated that about 10 percent of the adult population in developed countries has papilloma infections of the genital tract.

A number of HPVs have been linked with various precancerous lesions and malignant tumours, especially cervical cancers in women. In fact, one or more of these high-risk-type HPVs have been found in more than 90 percent of women diagnosed with cervical cancer. Their presence can be detected through an ordinary pap smear. The first vaccine against HPV was developed by Australian immunologist Ian Frazer. It was approved in 2006 by the U.S. Food and Drug Administration for use in girls and young women ages 9 to 26; it was sold under the trade name Gardasil. The vaccine is effective against HPV-16 and HPV-18 and thus can prevent most cases of cervical cancer in women who have never been infected with the virus. The vaccine is also effective against two low-risk strains, HPV-6 and HPV-11. Gardasil has also been approved for use in boys and young men. It is most effective when

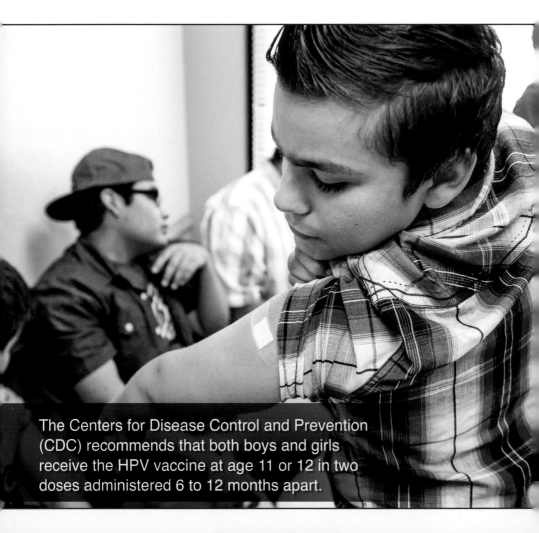

The Centers for Disease Control and Prevention (CDC) recommends that both boys and girls receive the HPV vaccine at age 11 or 12 in two doses administered 6 to 12 months apart.

given to boys and girls at age 11 or 12 as a series of two injections 6 to 12 months apart. Individuals over age 14 receive three injections within six months. Another vaccine, Cervarix, was approved in 2009 for use in girls and young women ages 9 to 25; it protects against HPV-16 and HPV-18.

Animal papillomaviruses can be transmitted in several ways and can cause a variety of warts and benign and malignant diseases. In cattle BPV can be transmitted from infected females to susceptible calves through skin contact during suckling or from bulls to females during breeding. Some cattle develop fibropapillomas, in which a wart contains both epithelial and connective tissues. Fibropapillomas are the most common type of benign growth found in cattle, sometimes occurring endemically on farms, and may be found on the head, legs, neck, penis, or teats. In the case of oral papillomaviruses such as COPV in dogs, warts may appear on the lips and spread to the tongue and the mucosal lining inside the oral cavity. In dogs with COPV these warts may sometimes become so numerous that they interfere with eating. Puppies with weak immune systems are most susceptible to COPV infection, though warts typically regress upon maturation of immune function. In rabbits infected with CRPV, warts may be persistent and become cancerous, causing squamous cell carcinoma. Warts usually appear on skin that is not protected by fur (e.g., ears, nose, and anus), which has led to the theory that the virus is likely transmitted to rabbits through the bite of an infected tick or other insect. CRPV can also be transmitted between rabbits.

PARVOVIRUS

A parvovirus is any virus belonging to the family Parvoviridae. Parvoviruses have small nonenveloped virions, and the icosahedral capsid is made up of 32 capsomeres measuring 18–26 nm in diameter. The parvovirus genome consists of a single-stranded DNA molecule.

Parvoviruses fall into two subfamilies: Parvovirinae, which infect vertebrates, and Densovirinae, which infect insects. Type species of the Parvovirinae include minute virus of mice, human parvovirus, and Aleutian mink disease virus. Whereas many species of Parvovirinae replicate autonomously, the genus *Dependovirus* contains viruses that replicate only in the presence of helper adenoviruses or herpesviruses; these strains are designated adenoassociated viruses (AAV). Densovirinae viruses are typically named for their insect hosts; examples include *Aedes aegypti* densovirus, *Bombyx mori* densovirus 5, and *Periplaneta fuliginosa* densovirus. Among the more widely known parvoviruses is canine parvovirus, which causes acute illness in dogs.

POLYOMAVIRUS

A polyomavirus is any of a group of minute onco-genic DNA viruses of the family Polyomaviridae. The virus was first isolated in 1953 when the murine polyomavirus was discovered to have caused tumours in laboratory mice. Since then the virus has been found in a wide variety of vertebrates, from green monkeys and baboons to cage birds (notably those of the parrot family, Psittacidae) and cows.

Two rare human polyomaviruses were isolated in 1971 and are known as BK virus and JC virus. Infection with BK virus may cause mild respiratory disease, whereas infection with JC virus can affect the respiratory system, the kidneys, or the brain. JC virus is responsible for causing progressive multifocal leukoencephalopathy (PMLE) in immu-nocompromised people.

Another example of a polyomavirus is sim-ian vacuolating virus 40 (SV40), which can infect humans, rodents, and monkeys. In some cases, SV40 infection in humans may lead to the growth of malignant tumours. The polyomavirus is highly antigenic, meaning that all animals bearing its tumours also have virus-neutralizing antibodies in their blood. The virus is also capable of clumping red blood cells and affecting DNA synthesis.

POXVIRUS

Poxviruses are members of the family Poxviridae. These viruses are responsible for a wide range of pox diseases in humans and other animals. Variola major isolates of the poxvirus species *Variola virus* were the cause of smallpox, which was declared eradicated worldwide in 1980. (Chickenpox of humans is caused by a herpesvirus.) The virus particle is somewhat brick-shaped, with the longest dimension as much as 250–300 nm. It is surface-studded with hollow spikes and contains DNA. Unlike other DNA-viruses, poxviruses appear to develop entirely within the cytoplasm of affected cells. The virus of rabbit pox, or infectious myxomatosis, has been used with mixed success in Australia to control the wild-rabbit population.

MAJOR GROUPS OF RNA VIRUSES

RNA viruses contain either double-stranded or single-stranded RNA, which may be segmented or nonsegmented and either positive-sense or negative-sense. A number of RNA viruses are pathogens of plants and humans. Among the latter are the retroviruses, which utilize reverse transcriptase for integration into host cell DNA, and the orthomyxoviruses, a group that includes the influenza viruses.

ARENAVIRUS

Arenaviruses are members of the family Arenaviridae. The name of the family is derived from the Latin *arenosus*, meaning "sandy," which describes the grainy appearance of arenavirus ribosomes (protein-synthesizing particles). Arenaviruses have spherical, enveloped virions that are 110–130 nm in diameter. The nucleocapsid, which consists of a protein shell (or capsid) and contains the viral nucleic acids, is helical and elongated. The arenavirus genome is made up of two segments of negative-sense RNA, and within the nucleocapsid are an endogenous RNA polymerase enzyme and small amounts of ribosomal RNA, which facilitate the transcription of negative-sense RNA into positive-sense RNA and the translation of the positive RNA into protein, respectively.

The arenavirus family consists of a single genus, *Arenavirus*, which contains more than 20 different species. Arenaviruses are widely distributed in animals and can cause serious disease in humans. The arenaviruses are evolutionarily adapted to specific rodent hosts, which generally show no signs of viral infection and thus act as reservoirs for the virus. Rodents excrete the virus in feces, urine, and saliva. When humans come into contact with food or soil contaminated by these rodent excreta, viral infection may occur, leading to disease. The arenaviruses cause the diseases Lassa fever (*Lassa virus*; occurring in West Africa), Argentine hemorrhagic fever (*Junin virus*), Bolivian hemorrhagic fever (*Machupo virus*), Brazilian hemorrhagic fever (*Sabiá virus*), and Venezuelan hemorrhagic fever (*Guanarito virus*).

BUNYAVIRUS

Bunyaviruses are members of the family Bunyaviridae. Bunyaviruses have enveloped virions that are about 80–120 nm in diameter. The nucleocapsid is helical and elongated. The bunyavirus genome is made up of three segments (large, medium, and small) containing single-stranded negative-sense RNA. The genome encodes an endogenous RNA polymerase enzyme that is used to transcribe the negative-sense RNA into positive-sense RNA, which can then be used for the translation, or synthesis, of proteins.

The bunyavirus family contains five genera: *Orthobunyavirus*, *Phlebovirus*, *Nairovirus*, *Tospovirus*, and *Hantavirus*. Most of these viruses are transmitted by arthropods (e.g., ticks, mosquitoes, and sand flies) and cause serious human disease.

Members of the genus *Hantavirus* cause acute respiratory illnesses in humans. The hantaviruses are rodent-borne viruses, each of which has been evolutionarily adapted to a specific rodent host. Human infection occurs where people come into unusual and intense contact with infected rodent populations, mainly through inhaling dust containing dried rodent excreta in and around the home but also in the wild.

There are several different hantaviruses, each with its specific rodent carrier, and they cause two basic groups of disease. The first group is known as hemorrhagic fever with renal syndrome (HFRS). These illnesses are characterized by acute fever, internal bleeding, and kidney failure. One of the first HFRS illnesses to be characterized was Korean hemorrhagic fever (also called hemorrhagic nephrosonephritis), recognized during the Korean War (1950–53). Korean hemorrhagic fever is fatal in 10 to 15 percent of cases. It is caused by the Hantaan virus and is carried by the striped field mouse (*Apodemus agrarius*), a type of wood mouse that is prevalent in Asia and eastern Europe. A second HFRS disease, nephropathia epidemica, is usually not fatal. It is caused by the Puumala virus, which is carried by the bank vole (*Clethrionomys glareolus*). Nephropathia epidemica has occurred in Scandinavia, western Russia, and other parts of Europe.

The second group of hantavirus diseases is hantavirus pulmonary syndrome (HPS), now recognized in a number of separate locations throughout the Western Hemisphere. HPS illnesses show a rapid onset of muscle ache and fever, leading to acute respiratory distress.

These illnesses are frequently fatal. The first HPS illness was identified in the southwestern United States in 1993. It is associated with a virus called Sin Nombre and is carried by the deer mouse (*Peromyscus maniculatus*). Other illnesses occur in Florida (the Black Creek Canal virus, carried by the hispid cotton rat [*Sigmodon hispidus*]), Louisiana (the Bayou virus, carried by the marsh rice rat [*Oryzomys palustris*]), Chile and Argentina (the Andes virus, carried by *Oligoryzomys longicaudatus*, a species of pygmy rice rat), and Central America (the Choclo virus, carried by *Oligoryzomys fulvescens*, another pygmy rice rat). Hantavirus infections are diagnosed by the symptoms, by a history of exposure to rodents, and by laboratory identification of antibodies to the virus circulating in the blood. Some cases have been treated with antiviral drugs such as ribavirin, but in most cases the focus is on controlling body temperature, fluids, and electrolytes. In severe cases the breathing is aided mechanically, and toxins are removed through kidney dialysis. Hantavirus infections can be prevented by controlling rodent infestations around dwellings, by washing infested areas with solvents and disinfectants, and by limiting exposure to likely rodent environments.

CALICIVIRUS

A calicivirus is any virus belonging to the family Caliciviridae. Caliciviruses have nonenveloped virions that are about 35–39 nm in diameter. They are icosahedral, with capsids composed of 32 capsomeres comprising 180 molecules of a single capsid protein. The calicivirus genome consists of single-stranded positive-sense RNA.

Caliciviridae contains four genera: *Lagovirus*, *Vesivirus*, *Sapovirus*, and *Norovirus* (Norwalk-like viruses). Type species of this family include *Vesicular exanthema of swine virus*, *Norwalk virus*, and *Sapporo virus*. Species of *Norovirus* frequently give rise to outbreaks of foodborne and waterborne gastroenteritis in humans. *Feline calicivirus* (FCV) is an agent that causes upper respiratory disease in cats.

CORONAVIRUS

A coronavirus is any virus belonging to the family Coronaviridae. Coronaviruses have enveloped virions that measure approximately 120 nm in diameter. Club-shaped glycoprotein spikes in the envelope give the viruses a crown-like, or coronal, appearance. The nucleocapsid is helical or tubular. The coronavirus genome consists of a single strand of positive-sense RNA.

Coronaviridae is generally considered to contain two genera, *Coronavirus* and *Torovirus*, which differ in nucleocapsid morphology, the former being helical and the latter being tubular. Coronaviruses are important agents of gastrointestinal disease in humans, poultry, and bovines. In humans, a species known as *SARS coronavirus* (or *Severe acute respiratory syndrome coronavirus*) causes a highly contagious respiratory disease that is characterized by symptoms of fever, cough, and muscle ache, often with progressive difficulty in breathing. The virus emerged in humans in 2002. It likely jumped to humans from an animal reservoir, believed to be horseshoe bats. The ability of *SARS coronavirus* to jump to humans undoubtedly required genetic changes in the virus. These changes are suspected to have occurred in the palm civet, since the SARS virus present in horseshoe bats is unable to infect humans directly.

FLAVIVIRUS

A flavivirus is any virus belonging to the family Flaviviridae. Flaviviruses have enveloped and spherical virions that are between 40 and 60 nm in diameter. The flavivirus genome consists of nonsegmented single-stranded positive-sense RNA.

Flaviviridae contains three genera: *Flavivirus*, *Hepacivirus*, and *Pestivirus*. Species of Flaviviridae are transmitted by either insects or arachnids and cause severe diseases such as yellow fever, dengue, tick-borne encephalitis, and Japanese B encephalitis. Well-characterized species of this family are the pestivirus *Classical swine fever virus*, the flavivirus

Yellow fever virus, and the hepacivirus of humans *Hepatitis C virus*.

Another well-known virus belonging to the family Flaviviridae is West Nile virus. Predominantly an infection of birds, West Nile virus is highly fatal for many avian species (e.g., crows and other corvids). A threat to human health occurs when infected birds are bitten by mosquitoes, which then transmit the virus to humans. Most human infections are inapparent or mild, causing a flu-like illness that usually lasts

Health officials collect samples of mosquitoes to test them for West Nile virus.

only a few days. However, in a minority of infected persons, particularly in those over the age of 50, the virus multiplies in the lymphoid tissue and circulates in the bloodstream (possibly also multiplying in leukocytes, or white blood cells) before reaching the brain, resulting in encephalitis. Symptoms of West Nile encephalitis include headache, fever, neck stiffness, disorientation, and muscle weakness. Death may result.

West Nile virus has been known and studied for decades, but historically it has been largely confined to Africa, the Middle East, and parts of Russia, India, and Indonesia, where it has caused occasional, usually minor, epidemics of dengue-like illness or sporadic encephalitis. However, the virus eventually was imported more broadly into Europe by migratory birds, and in 1999 it reached the United States, emerging in New York City, where it was detected in both birds and people. The virus subsequently was isolated from mosquitoes in Connecticut, and antibodies were detected in horses in Connecticut and New York. West Nile virus also spread into Canada and the Caribbean and, later, to most other U.S. states.

The number of bird, equine, and human cases in North America fluctuates annually. One of the most severe outbreaks in the United States was reported in 2012, when cases increased rapidly in late summer, particularly in the states of Louisiana, Mississippi, Oklahoma, South Dakota, and Texas.

There is no specific treatment for infection with West Nile virus. In severe cases, intensive medical care is necessary, with continuous monitoring of respiratory function, management of fluid and electrolyte balance, and prevention of secondary infections.

FILOVIRUS

Filoviruses are members of the family Filoviridae. Filoviruses have enveloped virions appearing as variably elongated filaments that are about 80 nm in diameter and generally between 650 and 1,400 nm in length. The virions are pleomorphic (varying in shape) and contain a helical nucleocapsid. The filovirus genome is made up of a single strand of negative-sense RNA, about 19 kilobases in length, and an endogenous RNA polymerase. The lipoprotein envelope of the virion contains a single type of glycoprotein, which projects from the virion surface and serves as the antigen that binds to receptors on host cells, thereby facilitating the process of viral infection. (Antigens are foreign proteins capable of stimulating an immune response in infected organisms.)

Filoviridae consists of two genera, *Marburgvirus* and *Ebolavirus*. The first strain of *Marburgvirus* was discovered in 1967, when it was transported with imported monkeys to Marburg, Germany, and

EBOLA OUTBREAK OF 2014–15

An outbreak of *Ebolavirus* ravaged countries in western Africa in 2014–15 and was noted for its unprecedented magnitude. By January 2016, suspected and confirmed cases had totaled more than 28,600, and reported deaths numbered about 11,300, making the outbreak significantly larger than all previous Ebola outbreaks combined. The actual numbers of cases and deaths, however, were suspected to be far greater than reported figures. The causative virus was a type of *Zaire ebolavirus* known as Ebola virus (EBOV)—the deadliest of the ebolaviruses, which originally was discovered in the 1970s in central Africa. EBOV was descended from ebolaviruses harboured by fruit bats.

The 2014–15 outbreak marked the first appearance of EBOV in western Africa (prior outbreaks involving the species had been in central Africa). Its newness to the region may have precluded the immediate identification of Ebola and use of precautionary measures by local physicians. Furthermore, most early cases of illness were characterized by fever, severe diarrhea, and vomiting—symptomology similar to that of diseases that had long been endemic to the region, particularly Lassa fever. As a consequence, EBOV circulated unrecognized for months in the Guéckédou and Macenta hospitals in Guinea, allowing for the establishment of multiple chains of transmission, distributed across multiple locations, to which the outbreak's unprecedented scale was later attributed. In

April, in hopes of facilitating its clinical recognition, researchers proposed the term *Ebola virus disease* (EVD) to describe the illness (EVD replaced the term *Ebola hemorrhagic fever*; hemorrhaging was not universal among victims in the 2014–15 outbreak).

A lack of local knowledge about EVD contributed to fear and mistrust among people in affected communities. As health care workers entered communities, donned protective suits, and established isolation units, from which few ill patients returned alive, fear intensified. Misunderstanding of the disease developed and was widespread in some communities. The severity of the outbreak also was a consequence of its emergence in countries with fragile health systems. National governments were unable to implement effective control measures. A lack of protective gear and resources for proper training contributed to numerous cases of illness among health care workers. Researchers also speculated that years of worsening poverty in southern Guinea may have forced people to venture deeper into forests for food and other resources, potentially bringing them into contact with bats that carried ebolaviruses.

The 2014–15 outbreak was the first large-scale Ebola incident to demonstrate potential for spread beyond Africa, a risk raised by high rates of international travel in the 21st century and by the presence of the disease in large villages and cities with mobile populations. (Previous outbreaks, by contrast, had been limited to small, rural, and relatively isolated villages.) Although WHO did not recommend general

(continued on the next page)

(continued from the previous page)

travel bans, which were thought to be relatively inef-
fective and have negative economic impacts, quaran-
tine measures were implemented for suspected cases
and for persons who had been in contact with infected
individuals. The identification and isolation of cases
and contacts in affected areas were the most-effective
means to stopping the outbreak.

As the outbreak slowed in early 2015, the extent to
which it had unraveled peoples' lives and devastated
local and national economies was becoming apparent. A
loss of manual labour had threatened crop harvests and
planting, raising concerns about food insecurity, while
the closure of borders, restrictions on travel, and declines
in manufacturing, mining, and foreign investment devastated economic growth. For people who had survived
Ebola infection, the transition back to their normal lives
was made difficult by social and economic challenges,
including being shunned by others in their communities,
and by long-term disability associated with post-Ebola
syndrome. The latter included visual problems, joint and
muscle pain, headaches, and extreme fatigue.

caused a fatal outbreak. The first strain of *Ebolavirus* was discovered in 1976, taking its name from the
Ebola River in the northern Congo basin of Central
Africa, where it first appeared. Type species include
the Marburg type *Lake Victoria marburgvirus* and
the *Ebola type Zaire virus*. Four other Ebola species have been characterized: *Reston ebolavirus*,

Sudan ebolavirus, *Ivory Coast ebolavirus*, and *Bundibugyo ebolavirus*.

Filoviruses are confined primarily to regions of central, eastern, and western Africa. They are among the most dangerous human pathogens known, causing highly fatal hemor rhagic fevers; some strains of *Ebolavirus* cause death in 50 to 90 percent of victims. The filoviruses may also cause disease in primates.

The origin of filovirus epidemics remains unclear. Marburg and Ebola strains have been found in different species of fruit bats. *Marburgvirus* has been isolated from the Old World fruit bat *Rousettus aegyptiacus*, which lives in areas throughout sub-Saharan Africa. This species is suspected to serve as a reservoir for the virus and may be responsible for outbreaks of Marburg disease in humans.

MYXOVIRUS

Myxoviruses are infectious agents belonging to the families Orthomyxoviridae (agents of influenza) and Paramyxoviridae. These viruses can cause the common cold, mumps, and measles in humans, canine distemper, rinderpest in cattle, and Newcastle disease in fowl. The virus particle is enveloped in a fatty membrane and is variable in shape, from spheroidal to filamentous, and in size, from 60 to 300 nm in longest dimension. It is studded with spikelike protein projections and contains RNA. These viruses react with mucin (mucoprotein) on the surface of red blood cells (hence the prefix *myxo-*, Greek for "mucin"); many of them cause red cells to clump together (agglutinate).

ORTHOMYXOVIRUS

Viruses of the family Orthomyxoviridae have enveloped virions that measure between 80 and 120 nm in diameter. The nucleocapsid has helical symmetry. The orthomyxovirus genome contains eight segments of single-stranded negative-sense RNA, and an endogenous RNA polymerase is present for the transcription of the negative-sense strand into a positive-sense strand to enable protein synthesis. The lipoprotein envelope of the virion contains two glycoproteins, designated hemagglutinin (major antigen) and neuraminidase.

Orthomyxoviridae contains four genera: *Influenzavirus A*, *Influenzavirus B*, *Influenzavirus C*, and *Thogotovirus*. The influenza viruses are known for periodically giving rise to pandemic outbreaks in humans. The infectious agents of bird flu are any of several subtypes of type A influenza virus. Other subtypes of this virus are responsible for most cases of human influenza and for the great influenza pandemics of the past. Genetic analysis suggests that the influenza A subtypes that afflict mainly nonavian animals, including humans, pigs, whales, and horses, derive at least partially from bird flu subtypes.

INFLUENZA OUTBREAKS AND EVOLUTION

Strains of the influenza A H1N1 subtype circulate constantly in human populations worldwide and thus are continually evolving and evading the human immune system. As a result, H1N1 is a major cause of seasonal influenza, which affects approximately 15 percent of the global population annually. In addition, since the early 20th century, H1N1 has caused several major epidemics and pandemics. The influenza pandemic

(continued on the next page)

Microbiologists at the CDC recreated the strain of H1N1 that caused the 1918–19 influenza pandemic in order to learn more about the virus and how to prevent and treat future outbreaks.

(continued from the previous page)

of 1918–19, the most destructive influenza outbreak in history and one of the most severe disease pandemics ever encountered, was caused by an H1N1 virus.

Other notable H1N1 outbreaks occurred in 1977 and in 2009. The 1977 H1N1 virus emerged in China and then spread worldwide. This particular outbreak primarily affected individuals born after the late 1950s. Older persons were believed to carry antibodies against a nearly identical H1N1 virus that had circulated in the 1950s. These antibodies appeared to cross-react to antigens on the 1977 virus, thereby providing immunity against the new strain. The 2009 H1N1 virus, called swine flu because the virus likely originated in pigs and contained genes from multiple strains of swine influenza viruses, first broke out in Mexico and subsequently spread to the United States and other countries around the world. In addition to the genes from different swine influenza viruses, the H1N1 virus that caused the outbreak was found to contain genetic material from human and avian influenza viruses as well. Thus, the virus is believed to have evolved through genetic reassortment that was presumed to have occurred in pigs.

Between worldwide outbreaks influenza viruses undergo constant, rapid evolution (a process called antigenic drift), which is driven by mutations in the genes encoding antigen proteins. Periodically, the viruses undergo major evolutionary change by acquiring a new genome segment from another influenza virus (antigenic shift), effectively becoming a new sub-type. Viral evolution is facilitated by animals such as pigs and birds, which serve as reservoirs of influenza viruses. When a pig is simultaneously infected with different influenza A viruses, such as human, swine, and avian strains, genetic reassortment can occur. This process gives rise to new strains of influenza A.

Newly emerged influenza viruses tend to be ini-tially highly infectious and virulent in humans because they possess novel antigens to which the human body has no prepared immune defense (i.e., existing antibodies). Once a significant proportion of a pop-ulation develops immunity through the production of antibodies capable of neutralizing the new virus, the infectiousness and virulence of the virus decreases. Although outbreaks of influenza viruses are generally most fatal to young children and the elderly, the fatality rate in people between ages 20 and 40 is sometimes unexpectedly high, even though the patients receive treatment. This phenomenon is believed to be due to hyper-reaction of the immune system to new strains of influenza virus. Such reaction results from the overpro-duction of inflammatory substances called cytokines. The release of excessive amounts of these molecules causes severe inflammation, particularly in the epithe-lial cells of the lungs. Individuals whose immune sys-tems are not fully developed (such as infants) or are weakened (such as the elderly) cannot generate such a lethal immune response.

Influenza viruses are categorized as types A, B, and C. The three major types generally produce similar symptoms in humans but are completely unrelated antigenically, so that infection with one type confers no immunity against the others. The A viruses cause the great influenza epidemics and pandemics, and the B viruses cause smaller localized outbreaks; the C viruses are not important causes of disease in humans. Influenza A viruses are classified into subtypes, and both influenza B and subtypes of influenza A are further divided into strains. Subtypes of influenza A are differentiated mainly on the basis of two surface antigens (foreign proteins)—hemagglutinin (H) and neuraminidase (N). Examples of influenza A subtypes include H1N1, H5N1, and H3N2. Strains of influenza B and strains of influenza A subtypes are further distinguished by variations in genetic sequence.

PARAMYXOVIRUS

Viruses of the family Paramyxoviridae have enveloped virions varying in size from 150 to 200 nm in diameter. The nucleocapsid has a helical symmetry. The paramyxovirus genome is made up of a single strand of negative-sense nonsegmented RNA. An endogenous RNA polymerase is present as well and is necessary for the transcription of the negative-sense strand into a positive-sense strand, thereby enabling proteins to be encoded from the RNA. The lipo-protein envelope contains two glycoprotein spikes designated hemagglutinin-neuraminidase (HN) and fusion factor (F).

Paramyxoviridae has two subfamilies, Paramyxovirinae and Pneumovirinae, each of which contains multiple genera. Examples of Paramyxovirinae genera include *Rubulavirus*, which is composed of several species of human parainfluenza viruses and the mumps viruses; *Avulavirus*, which contains the species *Newcastle disease virus* (of poultry) as well as various avian paramyxoviruses; and *Morbillivirus*, which contains the agents that cause measles in humans, distemper in dogs and cats, and rinderpest in cattle. Species of *Pneumovirus*, which are responsible for the serious respiratory syncytial virus disease in human infants, are classified in the subfamily Pneumovirinae.

Sendai virus, also called hemagglutinating virus of Japan (HJV), is an infectious agent of the genus *Respirovirus* in the subfamily Paramyxovirinae. Discovered in Sendai, Japan, the Sendai virus is naturally found in mice, rats, hamsters, guinea pigs, and pigs. The virus, which primarily affects the respiratory system, is highly contagious and is transmitted between animals via inhalation of contaminated air or contact with an infected individual. It generally only causes symptoms in animals with suppressed immune function, rendering the infected animal susceptible to secondary infection, which may be life-threatening.

The infectious particle reported to be the causative agent was first identified in humans from newborn infants that died of pneumonia in an epidemic in 1952. It is used in laboratory experiments to induce cell-to-cell fusion, to synthesize therapeutic antibodies, and to deliver DNA to cells in gene therapy.

PICORNAVIRUS

Picornaviruses are members of the family Picornaviridae, a large group of the smallest known animal viruses, "pico" referring to small size and "rna" referring to its core of RNA. The virus particle lacks an envelope, is spheroidal, measures from 20 to 30 nm across, and is covered with subunits called capsomeres. This group includes enteroviruses, which attack the vertebrate intestinal tract and often invade the central nervous system as well; rhinoviruses, which infect the tissues in the vertebrate nose; and the virus agent of foot-and-mouth disease. Among the enteroviruses are polioviruses, echoviruses (enteric, cytopathogenic, human, orphan), and Coxsackie viruses. Echoviruses cause fever with rash and meningitis. Coxsackie viruses cause sore throat or fever with chest or abdominal pains.

Rhinoviruses are capable of causing common colds in human adults and children. The viruses are thought to be transmitted to the upper respiratory tract by airborne droplets. After an incubation period of 2 to 5 days, the acute stage of the illness lasts 4 to 6 days.

REOVIRUS

Reoviruses are RNA viruses constituting the family Reoviridae. This small group contains primarily animal and plant viruses. The virions of reoviruses (the name is a shortening of respiratory enteric orphan viruses) lack an outer envelope, appear spheroidal, measure about 70 nm across, have two icosahedral capsids, and contain a core of segmented, double-stranded RNA. Characteristic features of structure, preferred hosts, and chemistry are the basis for dividing reo- viruses into several genera, of which *Orthoreovirus*, *Orbivirus*, *Rotavirus*, and *Phytoreovirus* are among the best known. Although orthoviruses have been found in the respiratory and enteric tracts of animals, they are not generally pathogenic in adults. Some orbiviruses cause disease in mammals (for example, blue-tongue disease in sheep); rotaviruses have been implicated in infective infantile diarrhea; and phytoreoviruses can destroy rice, corn, and other crops.

RETROVIRUS

Retroviruses are RNA viruses belonging to the fam- ily Retroviridae. These agents are responsible for certain cancers and slow virus infections of animals and cause at least one type of human cancer. They have also been identified as the cause of AIDS in humans, and they have been linked to one form of human hepatitis.

Retroviruses are so named because, by means of reverse transcriptase, they transcribe RNA into DNA. This constitutes a reversal of the usual cellular processes of transcription of DNA into RNA. The action of reverse transcriptase makes it possible for genetic material from a retrovirus to become permanently incorporated into the DNA genome of an infected cell and is widely used in biotechnology to synthesize genes.

HIV

HIV, or human immunodeficiency virus, is the retrovirus that causes AIDS. It attacks and gradually destroys the immune system, leaving the host unprotected against infection. The main cellular target of HIV is a special class of white blood cells critical to the immune system known as helper T lymphocytes, or helper T cells. Helper T cells are also called CD4+ T cells because they have on their surfaces a protein called CD4. Helper T cells play a central role in normal immune responses by producing factors that activate virtually all the other immune system cells. These include B lymphocytes, which produce

PREVALENCE OF AND TREATMENT FOR HIV/AIDS

According to data published by the World Health Organization (WHO), in 2015 about 36.7 million people were living with HIV, approximately 2.1 million people were newly infected with HIV, and about 1.1 million people died of HIV-related causes. Since 1981 about 35 million people have died from HIV infection. A 2014 United Nations report on AIDS indicated that between 2001 and 2013, however, the annual number of new infections in some 27 countries dropped by at least half, and since about 2005 the annual number of deaths from AIDS globally has also declined. The latter trend has been largely due to improved access to treatment for the afflicted. Thus, there has been an increase in the overall number of people living with AIDS.

About 70 percent of all infections occur in people living in sub-Saharan Africa, and in some countries of the region the prevalence of HIV infection of inhabitants exceeds 10 percent of the population. Rates of infection are lower in other parts of the world, but different subtypes of the virus have spread to Europe, India, South and Southeast Asia, Latin America, and the Caribbean. Rates of infection have leveled off somewhat in the United States and Europe. In the United States more than 1.2 million people are living with HIV/AIDS, and about 44 percent of all new infections are among African Americans. In Asia sharp increases in HIV infection have occurred in China and Indonesia.

(continued on the next page)

(continued from the previous page)

Access to antiretroviral treatment for AIDS remains limited in some areas of the world, although more people are receiving treatment today than in the past.

There is no cure for HIV infection. Efforts at prevention have focused primarily on changes in sexual behaviour such as the practice of abstinence and the use of condoms. Attempts to reduce intravenous drug use and to discourage the sharing of needles also led to a reduction in infection rates in some areas. Because HIV rapidly becomes resistant to any single antiretrovi-

A youth counselor at a community health centre in KwaZulu-Natal, South Africa, educates teens about how to prevent HIV and other sexually transmitted diseases.

ral drug, combination treatment is necessary for effective suppression of the virus. The variability of the virus and its rapid mutation also make it difficult to develop a vaccine for HIV. Clinical trials of HIV vaccines have had some limited success. Researchers announced in February 2017 that a therapeutic vaccine, intended to help patients keep HIV in check without having to take antiretroviral drugs, was showing promise in 5 out of 13 participants.

antibodies needed to fight infection; cytotoxic T lymphocytes, which kill cells infected with a virus; and macrophages and other effector cells, which attack invading pathogens. AIDS results from the loss of most of the helper T cells in the body.

HIV infects helper T cells by means of a protein embedded in its envelope called gp120. The gp120 protein binds to a molecule called CD_4 on the surface of the helper T cell, thereby enabling HIV to enter the cell. Once the virus has infected a T cell, HIV copies its RNA into double-stranded DNA by means of reverse transcriptase. Because reverse transcriptase lacks the "proofreading" function that most DNA synthesizing enzymes have, many mutations arise as the virus replicates, further hindering the ability of the immune system to combat the virus.

These mutations allow the virus to evolve very rapidly, approximately one million times faster than the human genome evolves.

Genetic studies have led to a general classification system for HIV that is primarily based on the degree of similarity in viral gene sequence. The two major classes of HIV are HIV-1 and HIV-2. HIV-1 is divided into three groups, known as group M (main group), group O (outlier group), and group N (new group). Worldwide, HIV-1 group M causes the majority of HIV infections, and it is further subdivided into subtypes A through K, which differ in expression of viral genes, virulence, and mechanisms of transmission. Genetic studies of HIV-1 group M have indicated that the virus emerged between 1884 and 1924 in central and western Africa. Researchers estimate that this strain of the virus began spreading throughout these areas in the late 1950s. Later, in the mid-1960s, an evolved strain called HIV-1 group M subtype B spread from Africa to Haiti. In Haiti this subtype acquired unique characteristics, presumably through the process of genetic recombination. Sometime between 1969 and 1972, the virus migrated from Haiti to the United States. The virus spread within the United States for about a decade before it was discovered in the early 1980s.

Pandemic forms of subtype B are found in North and South America, Europe, Japan, and Australia. Subtypes A, C, and D are found in sub-Saharan

Africa, although subtypes A and C are also found in Asia and some other parts of the world. Most other subtypes of group M are generally located in specific regions of Africa, South America, or Central America. The worldwide spread of HIV-1 was likely facilitated by several factors, including increasing urbanization and long-distance travel in Africa, international travel, changing sexual mores, and intravenous drug use.

SIV

SIV, or simian immunodeficiency virus, is an infectious agent of the genus *Lentivirus* in the family Retroviridae. The virus infects primates of the infraorder Simiiformes, which includes the so-called anthropoids—apes, monkeys, and humans.

SIV is transmitted through contact with infected body fluids such as blood. It is widespread among nonhuman primates, and in most species it does not appear to cause severe illness. In chimpanzees, however, SIV infection can cause a disease resembling AIDS in humans. Studies have shown that, similar to HIV, SIV infects helper T cells (CD4+ T cells). SIV-infected cells typically undergo apoptosis (programmed cell death) within one day of infection. As a result, the cells die more quickly than the immune system can replace them. Thus, immune function gradually deteriorates, giving rise to an acquired immunodeficiency syndrome, which leaves the animal susceptible to fatigue and potentially life-threatening coinfection with other organisms. The long incubation period before symptoms of disease appear underlies SIV's classification as a lentivirus, or "slow virus."

The SIV genome consists of a single-stranded RNA molecule that encodes only a small number of proteins, one of which is reverse transcriptase. In the form of reverse transcribed DNA, the virus can integrate itself into the DNA of the host cell's genome. Disguised as part of the host DNA, the virus can utilize the host cell's replication machinery to transcribe its DNA back into RNA, thereby creating a copy of itself. In this way, many new copies of the virus's genetic material are produced. The copies of SIVRNA are then packaged into new virus particles, each of which is about 80–100 nm in diameter. These particles eventually bud off from the host cell, a process that frees them to infect more cells.

Although all retroviruses are distantly related, there are very distinct similarities between SIV and HIV. Indeed, studies of their evolutionary origins have indicated that the simian form was a precursor of the human virus. The SIV jump to humans is believed to have occurred through the practice of butchering chimpanzees and other nonhuman primates for food. This increased the chances for viral transmission because it placed humans in contact with the animals' blood. Scientists suspect that once SIV was in humans it evolved into HIV via random mutation. The initial transmission of the virus from chimpanzees to humans appears to have occurred in Africa sometime between 1884 and 1924.

In 2009 a virus known as SIVgor, so named because it infects gorillas, was discovered to be very closely related to a newly identified strain of HIV-1. This discovery indicated that SIV had been transmitted from gorillas to humans.

RHABDOVIRUS

Rhabdo viruses are members of the family Rhabdoviridae. They are responsible for rabies and for vesicular stomatitis of cattle and horses. The virus particle is enveloped in a fatty membrane and is bullet-shaped, measuring approximately 70 by 180 nm. It contains a single helical strand of RNA.

TOGAVIRUS

Togaviruses are infectious agents belonging to any of three genera of arthropod-borne viruses (arboviruses) of the family Togaviridae. Flaviviruses, once considered to be of the Togaviridae, are now designated as members of a separate family, Flaviviridae. The togavirus genera are *Alphavirus*, which is carried by mosquitoes; *Rubivirus*, also called rubella, or German measles, virus; and *Pestivirus*, which infects only animals (hog cholera virus and bovine diarrhea virus). Some *Alphavirus* species produce severe encephalitis in humans. Horses also may be severely or fatally infected by equine encephalitis. *Rubivirus* is immunologically distinct from the other togaviruses.

Chikungunya virus is an infectious agent of the genus *Alphavirus*. The virus causes chikungunya fever, a disease that was first recorded in 1952–53 in an outbreak on the Makonde plateau, located on the border between Mozambique and Tanzania in Africa. The virus was initially isolated from a Tanzanian patient in 1953.

Similar to other alphaviruses, chikungunya virus is made up of a single strand of RNA that is about 12,000 nucleotides long. The RNA is contained within a capsid, which in turn is covered by an envelope.

A single chikungunya virion particle, which includes the capsid and envelope, is 60–70 nm in diameter. There are multiple strains of chikungunya virus, which differ from one another in their RNA sequences. These different strains are grouped within several distinct lineages of chikungunya virus, which are known as South/East African, West African, Central African, and Asian. Chikungunya viruses also have antigenic profiles that make them unique among viruses, including other alphaviruses. Antigens are proteins on the surfaces of virion particles that serve to promote viral infectiousness and to stimulate antibody production by the host's immune system. The antibodies generated and released into blood serum in response to chikungunya viral antigens enable these viruses to be detected by serological tests.

Nonhuman primates in Africa are believed to be the principal reservoir of chikungunya virus. The virus is considered enzootic in these animals—it circulates constantly in the African primate community but affects only a few animals at any given time. The virus is transmitted from its reservoir hosts to humans by arthropod vectors, the two known species of which are the mosquitoes *Aedes aegypti* and *A. albopictus*. The original vector of the virus was *A. aegypti*, which is native to Africa and India.

However, genetic mutations enabled viral adaptation to *A. albopictus*, which is native to Asia. This mosquito is considered an invasive species, and factors involving changes in climate and increases in human travel have contributed to the subsequent spread of the mosquito and the virus, respectively, to multiple parts of the world. Where *A. albopictus* and the virus are coincident, outbreaks of chikungunya fever are likely to occur. Thus, chikungunya virus has appeared in areas of Europe and the southeastern United States and on multiple islands in the Indian Ocean largely because infected humans traveled from areas where the virus was endemic to areas where *A. albopictus* was invasive. The ability of the virus to carry out its life cycle between vector organisms and humans has facilitated its sustained spread in these geographical regions, which are distant from its nonhuman primate reservoirs in Africa.

Chikungunya virus, similar to several other alphaviruses, is known for causing severe joint and musculoskeletal pain. Symptoms of illness appear 3–7 days after viral transmission by an infected mosquito. Although the disease is typically self-limiting— most symptoms disappear within 10 days—chronic arthritis, lasting months or sometimes years, occurs in roughly 10–12 percent of cases.

CONCLUSION

Since the first discoveries of bacteria, in the 17th century, and viruses, in the late 19th century, scientists have learned much about the features, classification, and evolution of these microscopic organisms and agents. Studying the diversity and genetics of bacteria can lead to breakthroughs in a wide variety of scientific fields. For example, the manipulation of bacterial genes for the production of genetically modified organisms such as crops is a rapidly progressing, though highly controversial, area of science.

Meanwhile, bacteria and viruses play a major role in disease, not only in humans but also in other animals and plants. The ability to anticipate which strain of influenza virus or Ebola virus will emerge next could enable countries to better prepare for and cope with epidemic and pandemic outbreaks. By isolating and identifying the agents that cause disease, researchers can begin to develop new treatments, perhaps even including vaccines to prevent viral diseases such as AIDS. The success of such medicines would prevent the suffering of many millions of people worldwide.

GLOSSARY

adenosine triphosphate (ATP) A molecule that stores and then releases chemical energy from food molecules. ATP is found in the cells of all living things.

autotrophs Organisms that use an inorganic compound, carbon dioxide (CO_2), instead of an organic compound, as their source of carbon.

bacteriophage A bacteria-infecting virus.

capsid A protein shell that forms a case around the nucleic acid in a virus.

chromosome A threadlike gene-containing structure of tightly-packed DNA and protein in the nucleus of eukaryotic cells.

cytoplasm The semi-liquid portion of a cell's interior.

deoxyribonucleic acid (DNA) A nucleic acid that contains the genetic instructions used in the development and functioning of all known living organisms and some viruses.

enzymes Biomolecules that increase the rate of chemical reactions. Nearly all known enzymes are proteins.

eukaryotic Describing cells in which the genetic material is enclosed within a nuclear membrane.

extrusion The process of pushing or forcing out.

flagella Thin filaments that some cells use for movement.

genome The entire genetic code of a living thing.

heterotrophs Bacteria that require an organic source of carbon to survive, such as sugars, proteins, fats, or amino acids.

interferons Proteins synthesized by vertebrates that inhibit the multiplication of viruses.

invaginate Folding something inward so that an outer surface becomes an inner surface.

lyse To break apart or destroy.

microbiology The study of microorganisms, or microbes, a diverse group of minute, simple agents that include bacteria, archaea, algae, fungi, protists, and viruses.

mitochondria Organelles contained in the cytoplasm of most eukaryotic cells that produce energy (adenosine triphosphate) for the cell.

nucleotides Molecules that, when joined together, make up the structural units of RNA and DNA.

obligate Essential for survival in a biological sense.

organelles Structures surrounded with enclosed membranes that are contained in a cell's cytoplasm.

pathogens Disease-causing organisms.

phenotypic traits Traits or characteristics that can be observed.

prokaryotic Describing cells such as Archaea and Bacteria in which the genetic material is not enclosed in a nuclear membrane.

ribonucleic acid (RNA) Nucleic acid structurally composed of ribose and phosphate units with uracil as a base rather than the thymine of DNA. RNA is critical to the process of protein synthesis as well as other cell functions.

transduction RNA complex compound of high molecular weight that functions in cellular protein synthesis and replaces DNA as a carrier of genetic codes in some viruses. RNA consists of ribose nucleotides in strands of varying lengths.

transposons Mobile genetic elements that can rearrange the order and presence of any genes on the chromosome.

virion A parent virus.

viroids Tiny disease-causing agents that consist of only a small circular RNA molecule, which lacks a protein coat.

BIBLIOGRAPHY

BACTERIA

A comprehensive survey of the vast array of bacterial species is presented in George M. Garrity et al. (eds.), *Bergey's Manual of Systematic Bacteriology*, 5 vol., 2nd ed. (2001–12), a reference and sourcebook accepted as standard throughout the world for classification of bacteria and related microorganisms. Advanced textbooks covering all general characteristics of microorganisms—including morphology, physiology, biochemistry, ecological role, and classification—are Michael T. Madigan et al., *Brock Biology of Microorganisms*, 14th ed. (2015); Joanne M. Willey, Linda M. Sherwood, and Christopher J. Woolverton, *Prescott's Microbiology*, 10th ed. (2015); and Lucy Shapiro and Richard Losick (eds.), *Cell Biology of Bacteria* (2011).

Thomas D. Brock, *The Emergence of Bacterial Genetics* (1990), describes the historical development of bacterial genetics and molecular biology. Additional coverage of the molecular and genetic features of bacteria is found in Larry Snyder et al., *Molecular Genetics of Bacteria*, 4th ed. (2013). Clive Edwards (ed.), *Microbiology of Extreme Environments* (1990); and Charles Gerday and Nicolas Glansdorff (eds.), *Physiology and Biochemistry of*

265

Extremophiles (2007), are detailed explorations of microorganisms that live in extreme environments. Bacteria in the human body and their role in human health and disease are discussed in Julian Marchesi (ed.), *The Human Microbiota and Microbiome* (2014).

VIRUSES

Descriptions of the diseases and their epidemiology are included in Bernard N. Fields and David M. Knipe (eds.), *Fields Virology*, 6th ed., 2 vol. (2013), a text on the structure, biological properties, replication, and immunology of virtually all human viruses of medical importance. David O. White and Frank J. Fenner, *Medical Virology*, 4th ed. (1994), is intended for medical students and other health professionals. *The Viruses*, 24 vol. (1982–94), a monographic series, critically analyzes in detail the biology, chemistry, and physical properties of each family of viruses—e.g., Bernard Roizman and Carlos Lopez (eds.), *The Herpesviruses*, 4 vol. (1982–85); and Jay A. Levy (ed.), *The Retroviridae*, 3 vol. (1992–94). C.H. Andrewes, *The Natural History of Viruses* (1967), offers a personal account by one of the pioneers in the field. Arnold J. Levine, *Viruses* (1992), a beautifully illustrated and well-written history and description of virology, provides insight into its scientific development. Sherwood Casjens (ed.), *Virus Structure and Assembly* (1985), contains an illustrated series of essays by some of the major contributors to the understanding of the physical principles that determine the structure and assembly of viruses. Abner Louis Notkins and Michael B.A. Oldstone (eds.), *Concepts in Viral Pathogenesis* (1984), *Concepts in Viral Pathogenesis II* (1986), and *Concepts in Viral Pathogenesis III* (1989), contain a detailed series of chapters by leading investigators on the disease-causing properties of many pathogenetic viruses. The international classification of the families, genera, species, and strains of all viruses discovered by 1991 may be found in R.I.B. Francki et al. (eds.), Classification and Nomenclature of Viruses (1991). Robert G. Webster and Allan Granoff (eds.), *Encyclopedia of Virology*, 3 vol. (1994), contains extremely well-annotated descriptions of every known virus in alphabetical order by common names with detailed indexes and tables.

Geoffrey M. Cooper, Rayla Greenberg Temin, and Bill Sugden (eds.), *The DNA Provirus: Howard Temin's Scientific Legacy* (1995), details Temin's research, his discovery of reverse transcriptase, and the influence and lasting impacts of his work. Neal

Nathanson et al., *Viral Pathogenesis and Immunity*, 2nd ed. (2007), provides an introduction to the interactions between the immune system and infectious viruses. Gail Skowron and Richard Ogden (eds.), *Reverse Transcriptase Inhibitors in HIV/AIDS Therapy* (2006), is a detailed survey of the pharmacology and development of reverse transcriptase inhibitors. Comprehensive coverage of the HIV/AIDS virus and disease is provided by Hung Fan, Ross F. Conner, and Luis P. Villarreal, *AIDS: Science and Society*, 5th ed. (2007).

INDEX